The Bridge Builder

An Ordinary Man with an Extraordinary God

SONNY JAYNES

The Bridge Builder: An Ordinary Man with an Extraordinary God

Text copyright © 2015 Sonny Jaynes All rights reserved.

No part of this book may be reproduced, or stored in a retrieval system, or transmitted in any form or by any means, electronic, mechanical, photocopying, recording, or otherwise, without express written permission of the author.

Unless otherwise noted, Scripture is taken from the New King James Version (NKJV). Copyright © 1982 by Thomas Nelson, Inc. Used by permission. All rights reserved.

ISBN: 978-1517089207

Published by Inkbug Media, LLC
Cover Design by Brian Jaynes
Interior Formatting by Jera Publishing
Printed in the United States of America

Endorsements

"An ordinary man does not build a fence for someone he DOESN'T EVEN KNOW out of pure kindness. An ordinary man does not take care of thugs, derelicts, and addicts that he doesn't even know out of pure kindness.

"You are extraordinary and anyone who knows you would JUMP at the chance to agree with me."

— Steve and Jeri Hill, Steve Hill Ministries

"When I met Sonny 40 years ago, God had already transformed him from a chiseled longshoreman to a humble servant who would cry freely when sharing about Jesus. It wasn't long before God multiplied the impact of his life. Through Gates of Life, Sonny readily became a spiritual mentor and father to those who were broken and wounded. Today, the influence of his life has continued to expand as his legacy has become secure. I am honored and blessed to know you, Sonny, as a fellow servant and friend. You are a treasure."

— Steve Harrison, author and director of B.U.D. Ministries

"The Bridge Builder is a refreshing and inspiring book. It is incredible what God can do with the life of an ordinary man. There are not too many men of God today that are an example to follow. Heb.6:12 says: "Imitate those who through faith and patience inherit the promises.

"Pastor Sonny's book clearly states, with his life story, the power available to ordinary people to see tremendous change in their lives through the hand of God.

"This is a book that will inspire you to seek and trust God, where God's presence and wisdom is tangible. A book of life written by God, revealing His wisdom and anointing. While you read, you will see the finger of God right the life of this "ordinary man." Don't miss it; you should have this book in your library."

— Rev. Alfredo Salvador, chaplain at Bradshaw prison, Henderson, Texas

"While reading "The Bridge Builder," I was reminded of many events and moments Sonny and I have shared during the 40+ years we've known each other. Heart-felt life experiences combined with nuggets of hard-learned wisdom flow freely from the pages of this book, presenting both challenges and encouragement to the reader. Throughout history we have seen evidence of ordinary people doing extraordinary things after a life changing encounter with the living God. Sonny may be an ordinary man, but his life story demonstrates what happens when an ordinary man surrenders to an extraordinary God."

— Robert Duran, missionary and director of Cave of Adullam Ministries

"The Bridge Builder" is a story anyone can relate to in their walk with the Lord. It speaks of God's faithfulness through years of walking out faith through real-life struggles. Sonny is open and transparent in his own struggles and yet glorifies the work of the Lord in his life. I appreciate the life of the man who could settle into retirement, but has chosen to finish "strong for the Lord." I think you will find this story inspiring and faith building in your own life."

— David Hickey, pastor of Community Christian Fellowship

"To know Sonny Jaynes is an experience that goes far beyond the "ordinary," despite the title of this inspiring book. For a while, I was blessed to have a front row seat to the life of this dear man and he impacted my life in an extraordinary way! As I walked with him I was encouraged by his character, challenged by his prayer life, propelled by his passion, and humbled by his tenderness toward the Lord. Sonny's leadership abilities that I witnessed went far beyond textbooks and classrooms. He truly displayed a life that has been impacted by the touch of God and the breath of eternity.

"As you read this book, you will most likely find yourself on some of the pages as I did. By this I mean that many of us grow up in settings that have a ring of the ordinary attached to our history. However, the ordinary turns into the supernatural when we, as Sonny Jaynes did, submit our heart and will unto Jesus Christ. At this stage, we enter the journey that defies the ordinary and opens up possibilities beyond our human reach and ability.

"Lastly, as you now explore the pages that spell out the life of Sonny Jaynes and his great God, I want to encourage you to glean from the history of this man whose life can be characterized by the words of the apostle Paul when he said in first Corinthians 15:10, "but by the grace of God I am what I am…"

— Keith Collins, director, Fire School of Ministry, Founder of Generation Impact Ministries

"I could never argue with the premise of this book, God does use ordinary men. Sonny Jaynes as he claims may be an ordinary man, but he has done extraordinary things. God used him mightily as his life has intersected with some extraordinary servants. It was my joy to work with Sonny at Brownsville Revival School of Ministry; Sonny and Margy became my friends. Even before I moved to Pensacola, Sonny caught my attention. I didn't know his name, but when my friends were headed to the revival, I would tell them to find a guy who looks like Lloyd Bridges and let him pray for you. I recognized that Sonny walked in a special anointing. Sonny is a man of prayer. He is a man of integrity. He is a man of wisdom. In a day of religious pranksters and shysters, Sonny practices what he preaches. My life is richer because I know him. You will enjoy this story of Sonny's life. You may not agree with Sonny on everything. If you're like me, you can't even agree with yourself at all times. You will agree with me on this, Sonny Jaynes, God's ordinary man, has been used in more than ordinary ways."

— Dr. Larry Martin, River of Life Ministries, Inc., Christian Life Book

"These pages contain true stories of courage, sacrifice, and transformation. Jesus says, "Greater love hath no man than he lay down his life for his friend." I have had the privilege of knowing

Margy and Sonny Jaynes for 25 years. Their commitment to the gospel—love in action— demonstrated daily by rescuing and parenting young men who were bound for jail and misery has been an inspiration to all who call them friends. This book tells where hidden work of true ministry—never seeking a public platform or popularity—but daily work of discipleship as Jesus commanded. They have been, and continue to be, models and mentors to me and those who have had the privilege of walking beside them. Beware, reading this book will ruin you, yet rescue you from comfortable Christianity."

— Paul Baloche, internationally known songwriter and worship leader

Acknowledgments

I'd like to thank Carol Scott, Patricia Bains-Jordan, Cynthia Ward and Carrie Pruett for all their help in editing this book. A special thanks to best-selling author Jennifer Jaynes for all her help with bringing this project together. Also a special thanks to my son Brian for cover design.

I dedicate this book to several people.

First of all, to my loving wife of 60 years who knows me more than anyone on the planet.

She knows of my struggles with anger and impatience as much as God. She knows my victories and my failures yet has loved me through it all. She has demonstrated unconditional love almost as much as God.

Secondly, I dedicate this book to all my children and grandchildren whom I love dearly and pray that they will read this book and be motivated to serve God.

Last but certainly not least, I dedicate this book to my Savior, the Lord Jesus Christ, who saved me from a miserable life of sin and gave me purpose for living.

Table of Contents

Forward 1
Introduction 3
1   The Early Years 7
2   Junior High School 15
3   The Marines 25
4   Korea 31
5   New Beginnings: Parents Saved 37
6   Salvation in Our Lives 43
7   New Challenges: Summer Camps 55
8   New Inspirations 65
9   Life at Coffee Grounds 79
10 The Beginning of Gates of Life 93
Photos 99
11 The Birth of Gateway Fence Company 109
12 Continuing the Journey: Changed Lives 123
13 Our Children 145
14 New Ministries 157
15 My Life, My Wife 171
Open Letters to My Children 173
My Core Beliefs 177
Books That Have Helped Define Me 201
In Closing 203
Lord, Light The Fire Again 205

Forward

WHAT CAN GOD do with an ordinary man? Watching Sonny Jaynes over these past 40 years is to see how much his great life has become an influence to so many men and women. His commitment, consecration, and just plain commodore common sense is an ongoing evidence of his own real test of faith. Sonny says, in his own biography, he is only "an ordinary man." To know him at all might make you question that analysis, though you could never doubt his truthfulness, humility, and honesty.

To look at him, you might instead mistake him for a well-known former movie star. To hear him speak or share with a crowd, perhaps some seasoned sea captain, famous pop singer or a serious night television host. To watch him work over the years both privately and publicly with troubled men and hurting families in so many different situations for healing and wholeness, you might see him as a counselor, a comforter, and a commander of confidence for a restored future that can be made real.

So—what can God do with the life of an ordinary man? Reach into his story and find out for yourself. He is indeed, in many ways, so like us all. Read the record of this one man. The answer may be a lot more than you think or ever expect to have happen. That's what those who have known him best also found in what he found. And it can happen to you.

Winkie Pratney
International Author and Friend
December 1st 2013

Introduction

"BY THE RIVERS of Babylon, there we sat down, yea, we wept when we remembered Zion" (Psalm 137:1). As I began to write my life story, it made me think of what I call "the good old days." My mind could go all the way back to the 1940s. I remember traveling down Main St., Houston, Texas, as a boy. You could hear the newsboys shouting out the headlines, "Read all about it.

Hitler invades Poland!" Or, "The Germans just bombed England!" Or even, "The Japanese just bombed Pearl Harbor!" World War II was vivid in my mind as I grew up. The nation united to stop Hitler and his totalitarian quest to conquer the world. It seemed everyone prayed. The country was beginning to recover from the Great Depression of the 20s and the early 30s. Popular items, such as coffee, sugar, and gasoline, were rationed and people didn't seem to mind, since it was to make sure our troops had what they needed. The people donated their aluminum pots and pans to help build warplanes. Mountains of pots and pans filled a section of Main Street in downtown Houston. We had war bonds to help with the expense of the war.

There were no selfish demonstrations in the streets to protest the discomfort of the war. We were a nation united.

Then came the 50s with rock 'n roll music and the Korean War. Times were beginning to change and usher in the 1960s with the Beatles, hard rock, drugs, and then the Vietnam War and the protesters. These protesters were usually pot-smoking hippies. Sodomy and homosexuality were felonies up to the 1960s. You could spend time in prison if caught in this kind of act. Then came the free-love revolution, sparked by the perverted mind of Alfred Kinsey, who himself was given over to sexual perversion. This was the "if it feels good, do it" philosophy that ignored God's laws that say, "Thou shalt not…"

David Wilkerson, the founder of Teen Challenge Ministries, predicted the open market of porn long before it happened. Then the Supreme Court ruled in Roe versus Wade in the 70s and abortion-on-demand became law, and many unborn began to be murdered. At about that time, Madalyn Murray O'Hair, who was later found cut to pieces in some barrels, gave enough voice that eventually got prayer and Bibles out of the schools while the church stood passively by and let it happen.

As I write this, we have the threat of Islam fast gaining a voice because of the 'politically correct' philosophy of the Liberal Progressives. We have a president that caters to the homosexual agenda and has passed laws that allow gays to openly flaunt their lifestyle in our military. He has also praised Muslims for their tremendous contribution to America. What have they contributed to make America great? 9/11! Three thousand innocent deaths! The only invasion of our country in 200 years!

There is a Babylon spirit in our country, and the church needs to rise up and be salt and light. No matter what the cost, we need God.

Now why all this, before I write this simple story of a no-name ordinary man? Because it is the ordinary people that God uses. The merchants, mechanics, bankers, grocery clerks, longshoremen, and all the simple people that have a personal relationship with God and are committed to be salt and light in this dark world. These are the ones that will turn America around.

"If my people who are called by My name, shall humble themselves and pray, seek, crave and require of necessity My face, and turn from their wicked ways, then will I hear from heaven, forgive their sins, and heal their land" (2 Chronicles 7:14 Amplified Version).

In the year 2013, we are under the leadership of a very liberal president. Our country is under economical and moral decline. It seems that we're headed in the direction that destroyed Rome and other civilizations. The late evangelist, Leonard Ravenhill, said, "America is too young to die."

So what will it take to bring revival and restore our nation? Ordinary people! That is what this book is about. "Give me one hundred preachers who fear nothing but sin and desire nothing but God, and I care not a straw whether they be clergymen or laymen, such alone will shake the gates of hell and set up the kingdom of heaven upon earth," declared John Wesley in a letter written in 1777.

As I continue with this introduction, I can look forward and see Christians today in the same light as the Jewish nation was during their captivity in the Old Testament. As they sat by the river, they remembered how it was before their captivity. There was joy and laughter! They were free to worship as they pleased. But they were unable to sing in this strange land. Seeing the changes from the early 40s to now, I can't help but think Christians may be in that same situation in the near future. We have been so concerned with material prosperity that we have followed men who promised ease, and have built on sinking sand. We seem to overlook the Scripture that says, "But seek first the kingdom of God and His righteousness and all these things shall be added to you" (Matthew 6:33).

I have been a Christian since 1958. I have never prayed for finances. I have always believed in giving God His tithes and offerings. God has always provided for me and my family. My concern is for the future of my grandchildren. I would love for them to live in the land of the free and the brave, but the current trend seems to be going in a different direction. I know that God gives a nation the government it deserves, so we must all pray for mercy. We must seek God with our whole heart. We must vote in free elections based on our Christian principles. I know a Christian government is not the whole answer, but I do believe we should get as close as we can to protect our religious liberty. God bless America!

"The true heroes of America are not the new Internet billionaires or the overpaid sports stars and movie actors or the wise guys who jack up their companies' stocks. The true heroes of America are the men, women, and teenagers who go to work for a modest wage, fulfill the responsibilities to their families and friends, and are kind and generous to others—because that's the right way to live…. The working people of the United States are the most important ingredient in the enduring American story."

— Excerpted from "Keep it Pithy" by Bill O'Reilly

CHAPTER 1
The Early Years

ON OCTOBER 24, 1935, at Jefferson Davis Hospital in Houston, Texas, a 9 ½ pound boy was born. His name was Claude Bennett Jaynes. (That's me.)

My parents were Claude Allen and Francis Jaynes. My mother was fifteen years old and my dad was nineteen when I was born. The hospital was a charitable hospital. Times were very hard, since the nation was just coming out of the Great Depression of the late 20s and early 30s. Work at the Port of Houston was slow and many struggled to survive.

My dad was a second-generation longshoreman. His dad, my grandfather, was a charter member of the International Longshoremen's Association, local 1273. He was at the Port of Houston when it opened in 1913. That port was the largest in the nation to be fifty miles from an open body of water. At the time of this writing, it is the third largest port in the nation.

Thirteen months following my birth my brother, Thomas Earl Jaynes, was born. We were to grow up together.

There's not a lot I recall about those first five years, but I do remember sketches of those early years. I vaguely recall an incident when I was about three years old. The boy that lived next door to us was about twelve years old, and he was bullying me one day. My aunt, who was my mother's sister, lived with us at the time. Her name was Bessiemae. She was standing on the porch of our house and saw what was happening. She immediately came to my defense. She beat the tar out of that boy. I don't remember him bothering me anymore after that.

We must've moved many times in those early years. I remember at least four moves during the first five years of my life. All of the places we lived were close to the port. I don't even remember having a car during those years. Times were very hard, and money was scarce.

I remember an incident when I was barely five years old. A neighborhood girl about my age and I were playing together in an old garage in the back of our rented house. I don't remember what led up to it, but we became curious about our private parts. So we proceeded to look at one another's. My mother caught us and I was taken into the house and given a serious whipping. I don't think either one of us knew what we had done, but we knew it was bad. I also recall a babysitter we had about the same time exposing herself to us. Why she did, we did not know. She was pretending to play some kind of game.

One memory that stands out about this time was rabbit hunting with my mom and dad on some old shell roads in Pasadena, Texas. Mom would drive the car while Dad sat on the fender with a shotgun. My brother and I would be seated in the back seat filled with excitement! The plan was that when Dad saw a rabbit, he would throw his hand up and Mom was to stop the car so Dad could shoot the rabbit. When Dad threw his hands up, Mom slammed on the brakes, and Dad went flying off the car. A barrage of cursing followed. Then Dad got back into the car and placed the gun in the back seat next to my brother's side of the car, just in back of my mom's head. She was driving the car. Of course the safety was not on and the gun was loaded. My brother Tommy became very interested in the gun as we proceeded down the road. All at once the gun went off! My mom shouted, "Oh, God, I'm shot! I'm shot!" Of course the only thing that was shot was a large hole in the top of the car that was not there before.

As I recall this story, it is funnier to me than a Three Stooges movie. But at the time of the incident, it was not funny to my mom and dad, or me and my brother. My poor brother received a serious spanking for something that was more Mom and Dad's fault than his. As I mentioned before, those were hard times financially. America was facing the Second World War and everything was rationed, including wages. My dad, a very hard-working man, always seemed to manage getting a job. Work at the Port of Houston was very slow, so my dad got a job at a local iron works. Since that was the beginning of the newly formed Federal Housing Association, Mom and Dad managed to purchase a home near where Dad worked. I believe the house cost $2,500. It had a small living room, a very small dining room, two bedrooms, and one bath. The kitchen was so small you could barely turn around in it. But it was home to us for years to come. My mom was very proud of that home. She always made sure everything was clean, and I do mean clean. We boys were not allowed to touch the walls for fear we would leave a mark.

Some of the best times I remember in my childhood years were our trips to our grandparent's house. They lived in a rural area with about two acres of land. The house was one big room. As you walked through the door, the first things you saw were twin beds. That's where Grandma and Grandpa slept. My brother and I slept on pallets on the floor. Then there was a large table in the middle of the room with a very small kitchen area to the right. They had no bathroom and no running water. Staying with Grandma was like being on a farm. For breakfast, Grandma would always fix large biscuits with eggs from her chickens. She also had a cow and a pig, and made her own butter the old-fashioned way. Sometimes my brother and I could help churn the butter.

Grandma had a dog named Spunky who had a curled tail. My brother and I would get Spunky to chase his tail. He would go round and round and we thought that was funny. I sometimes use this illustration in teaching about our quest for happiness.

Since my brother and I usually stayed on the weekends, we would go to church with Grandma. I can remember singing all the Sunday school songs like, "Come Into My Heart, Lord Jesus," or "Climb, Climb Up Sunshine Mountain." When church was over, we would go home and kill a chicken for dinner. I sometimes got to pluck the feathers after the chickens were placed in a pot of boiling water.

On the side of Grandma's house was a shed. Grandpa had a large chunk of black tar in that shed and I have no idea what he used it for. But my brother and I would sometimes cut a large piece of that tar and chew it like gum. Grandma said that it was good for our teeth. We had lots of fun at Grandma's. There were always a lot of neighborhood kids to play with. Those were some good old days I could never forget. No TV or cell phones or computers to distract us from playing outdoors.

Our grandmother's church was only about a mile from our house, so even when we were not at Grandma's house we would ride our bicycles to church on Sunday. Mom and Dad stayed home. They only went to church occasionally. None of us were Christians at that time.

When I was in the second grade, Mom and Dad took us to the movies to see, "Hitler's Children." It was a movie describing how Hitler indoctrinated the schoolchildren with Fascist doctrine. I told the teacher the story and she had me go to some of the other classes and tell them about the movie. That was my first experience at public speaking. By the time I was in the fifth grade, my brother Tommy was in school picking fights with some of the boys. The problem I had with that was he would always have them wait for his big brother at the bridge. The bridge was on the street that led to our house and that was where most of the fights were held.

An incident that stands out in my memory was when I walked home with one of the neighborhood boys and he picked a fight with me. As we fought, he started yelling for his mother. She came out and began to hold me as he proceeded to punch me with his fist. My mom happened to look out the door, and seeing what was going on, she quickly ran out and tackled that lady in the ditch. She was on top of her, while I had her son in the ditch punching him. I guess people learned not to mess with the Jaynes clan anymore. My mom was tough as nails and had a very short fuse. Some of this she passed on to me, as you can see as we continue on this journey.

The sixth grade was an exciting time as I recall. It was the custom that every spring they had a celebration called May Day. I don't recall a lot about it, but what really sticks out was the election of the prince and princess of the festival. I was voted Prince by popular vote. Of course the reason why I won was not because I was so popular, but because my mom and grandmother decided I should win. Since the votes were determined by the amount of donations that came in to the school, they saw to it that I would win. The princess was as wide as she was tall, and certainly was not a beauty. I reluctantly allowed a picture of her and me to be taken. Now let me say this about my mother and my grandmother. They loved me dearly, but they did not know the seed of selfishness that was growing on the inside. When I was about twelve years old, my mom and dad adopted a cousin who was not being cared for properly. Mom had taken the baby boy to watch while the mother and father were going through a lot of problems. Since Johnny was just a baby when we took him in, he was like my very own brother. We all loved him very much.

Kashmere Gardens was a very friendly neighborhood. There were lots of kids our age to play with. We would clean vacant lots and make our own football and baseball fields. There was no organized little league then, so we made up our own. Almost every day after school we would have a game going. Sometimes we would challenge other neighborhoods. My brother and I had bikes and we could ride for miles. One of our favorite things in the summer was a place called Dodson Lake. It had a lake with boats to rent and a big public swimming pool. It was approximately five miles from our home. So we rode our bikes there often in the summertime. We had a lot of unrestrained outdoor fun, quite different from today.

At twelve years old, I remember the strange feeling I had when I would get close to a girl. In those days, we had double-seated desks at school. I was in the sixth grade and was seated next to a girl named Ruth. She had freckles on her face, but I thought she was cute.

I remember learning to dance to "Put Your Little Foot." My first date was when I was twelve years old. I asked one of the neighbor girls to go with me to the movies. In those days, you could go to the movie and get a bag of popcorn for twenty-five cents. That included the bus ride. When we got to the movies, I asked her to lie about her age so we could get in for the children's fee. If you were twelve or older, you had to pay the full price. I earned some of my money by delivering Shoppers News. That was a paper we helped deliver early every Sunday morning. We had to be up by three in the morning and meet the manager at his house. I was usually the one to round up all the guys since I was the early riser.

One morning in particular is vivid in my mind. We were supposed to put the newspaper on the porch. As I approached one house, it was still dark. It was a large house with a big porch. The lights were on in the living room and the door was mostly glass. You could see inside the house. I looked in the door and there was a naked woman standing in the living room. I was scared speechless! I ran like a rabbit! That was my first experience to see a naked woman. If it had been a few years down the line, I would probably have lingered a little longer.

In those days, we always looked for ways to earn extra money. One of the jobs I had was selling the Sunday morning newspaper at a large railroad crossing where there were always cars lined up waiting to cross. As the cars lined up, we would go from car to car selling our papers.

Yes, those were the good old days.

As I said before, my brother and I had pretty much a free reign in the summertime, but it seemed that we went in opposite directions. He had his friends and I had mine. In the small neighborhood where we lived, an open field and a patch of woods ran alongside a large drainage ditch. We often camped out in the woods. Near to these woods was a dirt road where many lovers would come and park at night.

One night we decided to check out a car that was parked there. We hid behind some bushes and watched for a while. I had a large flashlight so I ran up to the car and flashed the light on the two lovers making out. Then I turned and ran like a rabbit and hid with the rest of the boys. The man quickly started the car and turned the headlights to face our direction. We were scared speechless! Since we were well hidden the guy soon left. Needless to say we never did that again.

Another incident I remember was stealing pears from a neighborhood pear orchard. A railroad track ran alongside the woods and crossed a large drainage hole where we would often go skinny dipping when it rained really hard. We discovered a pear orchard that backed up to the railroad just a short distance from our swimming hole. One day we decided to go and rob that orchard for pears. We managed to get a few pears before the owner came out with his gun and chased us off. We never went back there anymore. Life in those days was a mischievous adventure to say the least. But more was to come.

CHAPTER 2
Junior High School

OUR GRADUATION TO junior high school was an exciting moment for the sixth-grade class at Kashmere Garden Elementary School. We were headed to Marshall Junior High School. A lot of changes were going on in me as a 13-year-old boy. I was experiencing puberty and my assessment of the female population was changing.

That was definitely a time when I needed my parents to explain the changes that were going on. It was a confusing time. I began to focus on girls a lot. I think I was searching for genuine love, but the problem was I had no real example. My only resources were the romantic movies with their unrealistic idea of falling in love. I believe if a young boy needed anything it would be the need of a father to sit down and talk to him about the facts of life. He needs to explain to him about the changes taking place in his body. Now all of this is me looking back on life realizing this through years of experience and failures with my own boys.

My dad was not one to sit down with me and explain the changes that I was experiencing. So I took the path I call the Underground Explanation. There were some pornographic comic books that circulated all through junior and senior high. These were not as graphic as the ones today since they were cartoon drawings and not real pictures, but they certainly had a strong influence. I begin to notice the shape of a girl as much as their facial beauty and that became a source of fantasizing.

I got my first real job at thirteen years old with an old friend of my mom and dad. His name was James Brown. He owned a gas station and watermelon stand on Harrisburg Boulevard, just down the street from the union hall where my dad went every morning. That was very convenient for me so I could ride to work with my dad.

Brown paid me $25 a week during the summer to run the watermelon stand. That was a lot of responsibility for this thirteen-year-old. I bought all my school clothes the next summer and spent the rest on I don't know what. There was an incident that summer that taught me a lot about personal responsibility. The summers in Houston were very hot and the days could get very long. There was a large box containing ice-cold watermelon. The top of the box made a great, cool bed for an afternoon nap. So I would lie on top of it when things were slow. One day after a good nap, I woke up when a customer came in. After he bought a watermelon, I went to put the money in the box that was used for that purpose, and it was gone. It was late afternoon, so I worried about it until closing that night at 10 p.m. Since Mr. Brown's station was just across the street, we both closed at the same time. I did not know what to do so I just blurted out, "Someone stole the money box!" He looked at me with sternness and said, "I guess the money will have to come out of your pay." That devastated me since it was probably a couple of week's salary in that box. As we continued shutting down the business for the next half hour, I could not get it out of my mind. How stupid and irresponsible I was to leave that money box unattended. Well, after we finished closing, the owner came to me and said, "I took the box while you were sleeping to teach you a lesson on responsibility. I hope you learned a lesson." Boy! Did I breathe a sigh of relief! As far as sleeping on that box, that never happened again.

I had just turned fourteen when my dad began to get me jobs occasionally on the docks at the Port of Houston. There were not many boys at fourteen years of age who could throw 100-pound bags of rice and fertilizer all day. I also had a job at the local Houston Chronicle selling subscriptions to the newspaper. Of course working and making money caused me to pay less attention to school.

At that stage of life, I was smoking and hanging out with boys with questionable reputations and getting into a lot of fights. One fight I remember the most was with an Italian boy who was a bully. He would trip me when I walked by his desk in the classroom. One day I had had enough. We were in the gym and he made some smart remark and I slugged him. The fight was quickly broken up. When PE was over, we went to the locker room to get dressed. The fight started all over again. That went on every day at PE. He was a dirty fighter; he wore a handful of big rings so he could damage my face. He would also have his gang at the buses every day, hoping to catch me, but I worked downtown and didn't ride the bus.

I later enrolled at the high school by my grandmother's house to get away from some of the fights. That school was across town close to my grandmother's house. We could use her address to get me enrolled. I had to catch two buses to get to school every morning, but that didn't stop the fighting. I stayed there for one semester and then went back to Marshall Junior High School, where the fighting continued until I finally quit school.

I first met my future wife in the eighth grade. Of course, I never dreamed that we would later be married. I think I had one date with her, but we would pass frequently in the halls and speak. When we were in the ninth grade, the school newspaper came out with a prophecy that said, "Margy Boykin will soon be Mrs. Claude Jaynes." Well, that was more of a laugh at that time.

Graduation time came and the class moved across the street to Jefferson Davis High School. That was a very disappointing time for me because I had to stay at Marshall, which separated me from all my friends. Of course it was my fault, since I had lost all interest in school and made failing grades.

I need to mention something here concerning my brother, Tommy, who was constantly in trouble. He had run away from home several times and no one seemed to know what his problem was. One day he slipped out of the house in the night and was caught stealing a car. They sent him to the reform school in Gatesville, Texas. That place was like a prison, and it just made him even more bitter. I feel guilt now even as I write this story, that I did not realize what his problem was, but at that time I was living for no one but me. I had hardly any concerns for anything or anybody but me. Soon after he was released from the reform school, he got in trouble once again. So Mom and Dad decided to enroll him in a military school in San Antonio, Texas. It was a very expensive school that cost $900 per semester, plus uniforms. Mom and Dad did not know what else to do. Tommy was there for only one week when he ran away again. Now since they had already bought uniforms and paid tuition, they asked me if I wanted to go to the school to finish out that semester. So I entered Peacock Military Academy, and that turned out to be a very good experience for me. The discipline was just what I needed. I seemed to fit well in the military life. My grades improved and I finished that semester with a C average; a good improvement from the F's I usually made.

I really wanted to go back to the school, so Dad said if I would work at the docks that summer and help with the tuition, I could return to the academy. Well, I worked hard that summer, but I didn't save my money. I spent it on clothes and cars and good times, so naturally I had to return to school in Houston. In some ways that was good for me because, since I had passed the ninth grade in military school, I was then caught up with my schoolmates,. So I enrolled at Jefferson Davis High School, which made me feel really good about myself. I determined in my mind to put all my heart in my class work so I could graduate with them. The time in military academy helped me realize I needed to discipline myself to make good grades, but the excitement was short-lived. After two weeks, they called me in to the school office and told me the private school I attended had a different policy, and I would now have to go back to Marshall and repeat the ninth grade. That had a devastating effect on me and I wanted to give up on school. I turned to partying and drinking a lot. I managed to finish the ninth grade and finally was back at Jeff Davis.

Right after my experience with the military school, I became interested in singing. I had been in the school choir and had a fairly decent voice. I began to take voice lessons from a lady who taught voice in her apartment in downtown Houston. Her name was Mrs. John Wesley Graham. Her husband owned a hat manufacturing company in Houston and also one in New York. She promoted the Metropolitan Opera and had trained some very popular singers. She wanted me to sing opera, but I wanted to sing like Tony Bennett and Johnny Ray who were popular at that time. Since Mrs. Graham had her own radio program, I was able to occasionally sing on the program. One night Margy, my future wife, was on a date with a guy, and as they drove through downtown, they heard me singing on the radio. Margy said to her date, "That sounds like Claude." When I had finished singing, they announced my name and, much to their surprise, it was me.

Sometimes I was able to sing at the Veterans Hospital. They had a large auditorium and they would hold variety shows to entertain the troops. On one occasion when I sang, there was a young man who had a small orchestra playing at the event. He seemed to like my singing, so he asked me to come to the University of Houston where he played for a dance every Friday night. I went to the school, but for some reason I did not get to sing that night. It was probably just as well, since I had never sung with an orchestra before and I had no rehearsal.

At that time, I was struggling with sexual matters. While writing this book, I listened to a lady on Focus on the Family sharing some of her problems as a teenager. Her story reminded me of an incident that happened to me when I was 16 years old. I have never told anyone about this, but that lady gave me the courage to open up and share my experience. A friend that lived in my neighborhood and I decided to go hunting one day. He knew someone who had a cabin on a game reserve near Houston. We decided to go there and spend the night and try to kill some hogs or deer. He also had an older brother who had been released from prison not too long before this happened. He went along with us and seemed very nice and well-mannered, so I did not think too much about it. When we went to bed that night, I ended up in a double bed with that older man. My friend slept on the couch. During the night, that man attempted to molest me. That being my first and only encounter with that kind of thing, I could not respond to his aggressive approach. Although at that stage in my life I was experiencing a lot of fantasies about sex with women, I had never once thought about that with a man. I left that night feeling guilty about allowing it to go as far as it did. I kept it inside and never said anything to anyone about the matter. Since I am much older now and have worked with homosexuals and those who are adulterous, I've learned that freedom can come when we find someone to share with—someone we can trust. In ideal circumstances, it should be our father. The Bible says, "For though you might have ten thousand instructors in Christ, yet you do not have many fathers…" (1 Corinthians 4:15).

After many failures in my life with my own children, let me offer this advice. A dad should be the kind of father that his children can trust with anything—not a reactionary, but a good listener; always responding with kindness and understanding. This is something that needs to start from birth. It has taken many years for me to learn this. As the old gospel song said, "I don't want to go back to my old life." One other thing to think about: don't blame your father for your sins. Change came to me when I realized that although my father had a strong influence on my life, he certainly was not the cause of my sins. Everyone will be held accountable for their own sins.

One thing I failed to mention was, shortly after military school, Mom and I bought a 1948 Chevrolet Fleetwood together. It was a nice car. I spent $500 one summer fixing it up. I had it painted black with a new paint called synthetic enamel. I had all the chrome taken off, including the trunk latch which was operated from the glove compartment. I also had the interior custom made from yellow and black quilted plastic—a popular material during that time and cheaper than leather. Everything including the door panels was of the same material. I was about 16 years old when I got that car, and I thought I was hot stuff.

At about the same time, I met the first girl I went steady with. She was a little younger than I was, but since I had been put back a year in school we were in the same choir class. It was what they called puppy love. They say puppy love is real to a puppy. I'm not sure how long we went together, perhaps six months. One day she told me she didn't want to go with me any longer, and that broke my heart. Shortly after breaking up with that girl, I was out with my best friend and his girl. We had been to a dance in a local park and recreational facility. My friend and I had been drinking. As we pulled out of the park, I made a wide turn and crashed into a telephone pole. Thankfully, I was the only one hurt. My friend and his girlfriend hid behind some bushes while they hauled me off to the hospital. They later called her mom to come and pick them up.

At the hospital, while I was in bed with a large gash on my forehead, I overheard my mom talking to the police officer outside the door. She said, "Oh, Officer, my son doesn't drink." I then yelled out, since I was still quite goofy from the liquor, "Oh, yes, I do!" Well, that was the end of my beautiful car. It was totaled out and I never had another one after that while in school.

Sixteen proved to be a very confusing time in my life. I had no motivation for anything but having what I then called a good time. It seemed that while Mom and Dad focused on my brother and his problems, thinking I was doing all right, I had a lot of unrestrained freedom to explore the world of sin. It was at that age I had my first experience with sex. Some of my friends and I went to Galveston to some places on Post Office Street. The street had a whole row of houses of ill repute. I had never seen anything like it before. There was an open bar in every house and they never asked for IDs. You could buy drinks while searching out the girls. The place was full of scantily clad young girls hanging around to entice you. They wanted you to buy sex from them. Most of these girls looked about my age, and most were very attractive. Shortly after that, the Texas Rangers closed those places down.

Just before I turned 18, my friends Joe and John Curtis, who were identical twins, approached me about joining the Marines. So as soon as I turned 18, we all signed up to join the US Marines. Since I had no real direction in my life, I decided I would sign up for four years and make it a career. Joe and John signed up for three years.

Just before leaving for the military, Margy, my old friend from junior high, called me and invited me to a Sadie Hawkins dance at the high school and we became acquainted once again. I thought she was a very attractive girl and a good person to be with. We seemed to enjoy one another's company. I asked her for her address so I could write her while in boot camp.

CHAPTER 3
The Marines

WE ARRIVED AT the Marine Corps Recruiting Depot in San Diego the day before the Marine Corps' birthday, November 9, 1954. The next morning we went to the mess hall and had a great breakfast. We also had a very good evening meal and everything was kind of laid back all day. I thought to myself, this is not going to be very bad at all. Boy, was I in for a surprise!

The next morning, we were awakened at 6 a.m. and the very first words we heard from the drill instructor was, "All right, you feather merchants, fallout." While in the formation he spouted off, "I am going to teach you to hate your mother." He then told us that the pogie bait machines were off-limits. Pogie bait is the Marine Corps term for sodas and candy. He also informed us to write our mothers and tell them not to send us any pogie bait in the mail.

The main drill instructor was a staff sergeant. He was nice looking, but surprisingly short. We also had a corporal and a private first class who were the sergeant's assistants. We marched to the clothing warehouse to receive an issue of clothing. After that we were marched to the barbershop where they shaved off all of my beautiful blonde hair. I officially become a skinhead.

Bedtime also proved to be very interesting. When it was time to go to bed, a drill instructor would come and order us to stand by our beds. We then would be ordered to go to bed by the numbers. Each number represented a stage in which we would be asleep. When we got to number 10, we were to be asleep. In order to try to trip us up when he got to number 10, he would say, "Is everyone asleep?" If there was no answer, he would repeat the question. After a couple of tries he made this statement, "You better answer me."

One of the twins said, "Yes, sir!" The drill instructor then said," How can you be asleep and answer me?" He ordered us out of the bed to go through the same routine again. I thought that was so funny that I laughed almost uncontrollably. The drill instructor came to me and looked me in the face and said, "Jaynes, you think that was funny?" I said, "Yes, sir." He then said, "Well, laugh." He began to laugh with me and as he laughed he placed his hands on top of the bunks that were on both sides and kicked me as hard as he could in the stomach. My humor ended abruptly because of the intense pain and loss of breath. We all learned a serious lesson at my expense.

Another situation I remember well was at Camp Matthews where we learned to shoot the rifle. It was close to Christmastime and I received a large package from my mom. If you recall, at the beginning of boot camp, they told us to tell our mothers not to send any packages with goodies in them. I guess my mother thought that since it was Christmas it would be okay. So she sent a large package with homemade cookies and candy.

The drill instructor loved to tease us. He would let us see what we had gotten before he threw it away. At that time, Joe and John were squad leaders. They were the ones who took the packages to the dump, and they secretly held some back for me. What good friends they were!

Another vivid memory happened at boot camp while we marched in formation. The drill instructor gave the command, "Inspection arms." That meant we were to open our bolts for inspection. Then he would give the order to close the bolts. It was to be done altogether as one unit. Well, my bolt got stuck so I was late closing mine. The drill instructor came up to me and said he was going to show me how to close my bolt. He opened the bolt and told me to hold the rifle with the left hand. He then told me to place my thumb inside the chamber. I did as he ordered. He then told me to drop my left hand. When I did as he commanded, the thumb that was in the chamber was ripped open and I stood there with blood dripping off my thumb. The drill instructor looked at me and said, "I like blood." Everything in me wanted to hit that little squirt, but I kept it in.

Another event I remember happened at the end of boot camp. Everyone turned in all their gear that day while I had guard duty. I was guarding all the laundry hanging on the clothesline. Someone was supposed to relieve me so I could turn in my gear. Well, the day went by and no one came to relieve me. I went to the drill instructor's quarters and asked permission to speak to the drill instructor. That was the routine we had to follow to be heard. He gave me permission to speak so I told him why I was there. He then asked me if I had left my post. Of course I had to say that I had. He then punched me in the mouth. It busted my lip and once again I was bleeding. Everything in me wanted to hit that little bully, and although I was not a Christian at the time, I had learned a little about self-control. If I had hit him, I would have faced time in the brig.

Boy, was I glad when boot camp was over. After graduation, we were given a 30-day furlough prior to combat training at Camp Pendleton. My 30 days at home were spent mostly with my family and my future wife, Margy. During that time Margy and I became engaged. My mom strongly encouraged the engagement, because she really liked Margy. She thought Margy could help straighten me out, and she was partly right. Since Margy was so attractive, it was not hard to convince me that she was the one for me. We both agreed at that time not to get married until I returned home from overseas.

Well, here I was at Camp Pendleton in the mountains of Southern California. What a rugged place to begin combat training. Every day climbing up and down mountains with a full pack and a 9 ½-pound rifle got you in shape quick. There was not much energy left for anything else. I think a couple of weekends we hung out at The Pike at Long Beach. The Pike had a carnival-like atmosphere. There was a roller coaster and various other rides and games, plus a dance hall where you could pay a fee and find someone to dance with. I loved to dance and they had a fairly good orchestra.

After combat training, we went to the staging area where we were to await our journey to South Korea. One night I came in about midnight and I had just settled down to sleep when the officers on night duty came in and told me to go to the Red Cross. When I got there, they informed me that my brother, Tommy, was killed in an automobile accident. They had prearranged a round-trip ticket to Houston and a 20-day emergency furlough for me.

As I mentioned before, my brother had a very troubled youth. He was constantly in trouble with the law. He had spent time in the reform school and Mom and Dad tried everything they knew to help him. We all were ignorant of what his problem was. When he was 16 years old, he met a young Baptist minister who took an interest in him. He led him to a salvation experience with God. There seemed to be a tremendous change in his life at that time, but the rest of the family did not seem to embrace it. There were too many problems in our own lives. We mocked and made fun every time he made a slip. We were blinded by our own disbelief.

When Tommy turned 17, he joined the Coast Guard Reserve. I think he was happy for the first time in his life, but he was still rejected by the family. I have since come to understand what Tommy's problem was. My mom and dad gave all the attention to me and left Tommy sadly neglected. He needed some of the same love they showed me. I realized, even though it wasn't my fault, I could have been more sensitive to my brother's needs. I think the revelation that God gave me about my brother's rejection has led me into the ministry of helping troubled youth.

Well, here I was in Houston again, this time attending my brother's funeral. Since he was in the Coast Guard Reserve, he had a military funeral. It was a very nice funeral. For once, Tommy received the attention he always needed. I did not even weep at the funeral, but I have wept many times thinking about it since.

After a short while at home, Margy and I decided to go ahead and get married while I was in Houston. We had a simple wedding in my aunt's house. The guests included Margy's mother, my mother and dad, my aunt and uncle, my best man Conrad, and his wife Joyce, and, of course, the preacher. Since we had no money, my dad gave us $50 for our honeymoon. We spent one night at a hotel in Houston and then went on to Galveston. We were together only four days before I had to go back to California to await our voyage to Korea.

CHAPTER 4
Korea

THE TRIP OVERSEAS was on a huge troop ship. That was quite an experience in itself. The bunks, if I remember right, were four or five bunks high. I don't remember which one I was on, but I know it was high.

I quickly volunteered to help the ship's master-at-arms, a petty officer on the ship in charge of maintenance. My job was to report to him every morning after breakfast. His office was somewhere down below in the lower part of the ship. It was away from the rest of the troops, and that was good. He had very little for me to do, so I just hung around the shop.

Sometimes I would lie on the deck and sleep. I was glad to be away from the sickness on the ship. Fortunately, I never got seasick. At night, we would have a poker game in the head (bathroom). Sometimes we stayed up past midnight gambling. I was pretty hooked on gambling. My mom had poker games at our house in the daytime while Dad was at work, so I learned to play poker at an early age. Even in high school, we would shoot dice or pitch quarters to the line before school started every morning. Gambling seemed to flow in my blood. I understood that my grandfather was a gambler and an alcoholic. It took us about two weeks to get to Japan; it seemed like a month. We got our first chance to get off the ship in Osaka. That was my first experience in a foreign country. I remember riding all over town in what they called a rickshaw. It fascinated me that a little Japanese man could run and pull that thing all over town, with two and sometimes three Marines in it. They had to be in excellent shape.

After a short visit there, we headed to Korea. I don't remember how long it took, but I know it was not very long. We landed in Inchon and from there headed up close to the North Korean line. By that time, all the shooting was over except for an occasional outbreak. The base I was on was close enough to North Korea that we could see the North Koreans from any high point. My first job in the first camp was also my first experience at running a jackhammer as we dug a latrine. Some of my loneliest times were walking guard duty at night. I would think about how far from home I was and how much I missed everyone, especially my wife.

At the first camp, I was able to hook up with an old friend, Manny, from Kashmere Gardens. Joe and John had been separated from me after combat training, so it was good to see a familiar face. Manny Campbell was a little short guy with a big booming voice. We went on liberty together. Of course, our time on liberty was not spent in pursuit of God. I am too ashamed to write many details of what happened.

One occasion that stands out at that first base was breakfast the first morning. Since it was on the weekend, we had a very good breakfast. As I approached the part of the line where they were cooking eggs, the mess sergeant asked me how many eggs

I wanted. I thought he was kidding since no one had asked me before, so I said, "Give me a dozen." He gave me a dozen fried eggs and said, "I will be watching to see that you eat every one of those eggs." Sure enough, he was standing by the back as I was leaving to see if I had eaten all the eggs. I learned then not to smart off to the mess sergeant.

We were at that base just a short time before we were moved to another base further toward the coast, and it was at that camp that I became very ill. We arrived at the camp just before the monsoon season, and while we were out on maneuvers it began to rain. We were soaked down and I woke up the next morning with a temperature of 104. My sides hurt so bad that it felt as if my ribs were broken. I went to sick bay, and they told me I had double pneumonia. They said to put some things together so they could take me to the hospital—at least that's what they called the compound of several temporary buildings, looking nothing like our modern hospitals. On the way there, they had me riding in the back of a small-weapons carrier. The roads were rough and I was in so much pain that I banged on the back window until they stopped. I told them I could not ride in the back of that vehicle, so they had the corporal trade seats with me. They kept me in the so-called hospital for two weeks. When I recovered, they sent me back to the camp. It was really rough being there during the rainy season. We could never get our clothes dry. Every morning we had to put on damp clothes.

Fighting seemed to follow me wherever I went. I guess it was the short fuse I inherited from my mother. One of the incidents I recall was while we were drinking in what the Marines called the slop chute. That was the Marine Corps' name for the canteen. We had been drinking quite heavily since that was about the only thing there was to do. A corporal in our group was kind of a smart aleck. We got into an argument and decided to go outside and settle it. Since both of us were drunk, there seemed to be no winner. After that fight with the corporal, we seemed to get along pretty well.

Another incident happened while we were returning to the base from a day of partying in Seoul. We rode in the back of a large troop truck with about ten other men and we were all singing the "Marine Corps Hymn." Everybody got gung ho when they were full of booze.

One guy, who was always a know-it-all, refused to sing with us, so I proceeded to make him sing. I had him down in the back of the truck with his face on the bed. There was a broken bottle on the floor, and his face got cut a little from being pushed onto the shards. Well, they stopped the truck and we all got out. The guy I was fighting told the sergeant in charge that I had cut him with a knife. It was a bold-faced lie, because I didn't even have a knife, but I had to go before the captain who was in charge anyway. The captain was an older, more mature guy. I thought he was a very wise person, and he talked to me like a father to his son. He told me how childish I was to get in a fight with another Marine when we were at war. I felt like crawling under the desk. I took what he said and told him I was very sorry for acting so immature. He put me on probation and restricted me from liberty for a while.

Shortly after that, we went on maneuvers. They took us to Inchon where we waited a couple of days before boarding the ships that would take us out to sea. They gave the company leave to go into town on our first night there. The gunnery sergeant was a very nice guy and I think he liked me. I talked him into letting me go into town with the guys. Well, I got drunk that night and missed the bus that was to take us back to the base. I ended up having to hitch a ride. Another guy with me said he knew the guy on guard at the gate and that we could just walk in. Now there was a curfew and being out past that time was the same as being AWOL. As we passed the gate, the guard told us to halt. The guy with me said to ignore the guard, so we kept walking. Then we heard the guards say, "Halt or I will shoot." I knew we were in trouble. Apparently, either my friend lied or his friend was not on duty. We got stopped and I was in trouble with the sergeant. Once again he gave me another chance.

He told me that if I would be a good soldier and not get into any more trouble while on maneuvers he would not report me to the captain. Needless to say, I was a perfect soldier during all of our exercises. That lasted two weeks.

Another incident that happened while at camp sounds kind of funny. We had gone across the rice patty to the slop chute. Once again, I had too much to drink. We got back to the tent and I didn't make it to bed. I laid my head on the table in the middle of the tent and went to sleep. Someone had been painting something and they had left blue paint on the table. When we fell out the next morning for formation and roll call, I had blue paint all over my face. The sergeant asked me, "Jaynes, what in the world happened to you?" I replied, "Just call me Little Boy Blue." The whole squad burst out in laughter, including the sergeant. The laugh was on me though. Many incidents like that happened while overseas, but I am too ashamed to mention them all.

After being there for a few months, we soon got the orders that we were to help the 25th Army Division move out back to the states. We spent several weeks tearing down old Quonset huts and shipping them out. They were given to the Marine Corps. It seemed that the Marines always got the Army's left overs.

Not long after that, we got the orders for the First Marine Division to move out. Since I was in shore party, we had to load up all the equipment for the whole division. We were the last ones to leave Korea. Our trip back to the states seemed a little quicker. It was good to be home again in the good old USA.

During my last days in Korea, my wife had quit writing me and I found out why when I got home. She had divorce papers waiting for me. Since we had no children and had only spent four days together I decided not to contest it, but there was a nagging thought in the back of my mind that told me God hated divorce. I believe my grandmother, who was a Christian, told me so.

I was home for several nights and had no contact with my wife. Then one night, as I drove on Main Street in Houston on my way to a movie with a bunch of my old buddies, I saw my wife standing on a corner, waiting for the bus. I told the guys to stop and let me out to talk to her. We talked for a short while and I found out why she wanted a divorce. She didn't like my mother, because she tried to run her business. We decided to meet at the park the next day and talk things over. A lot of people need to talk things over before getting a divorce. After talking, we decided to forgive one another for any wrongs that were done between us. We also committed to one another to never bring up anything from the past when we got into arguments. We have kept that promise ever since that night.

CHAPTER 5
New Beginnings: Parents Saved

SOMETHING RADICAL HAPPENED after my brother's death. My mom and dad got saved! That happened at the little Assembly of God church where Grandmother Jaynes went. After my parents got saved, my aunts and uncles and cousins turned their lives over to Jesus. I guess the death of my brother shocked everyone into reality. Mom and Dad and all my relatives began to pray for my salvation.

Life was certainly different in the Marines with my wife there. After Margy arrived in Oceanside, California, we had to get a place to live. The first place we had was a rented room from an officer's alcoholic wife. She had wine in her refrigerator all the time. We shared the kitchen with her, and Margy and I had a bedroom.

For some reason, that period of time is a little vague. The incident that I recall the most was when our landlady lent us her car so we could go out one night. That was the nicest thing

I remember about her. She had a fairly new Pontiac and Margy and I had no car, and it was nice to be able to go out. We lived with her a month when we decided we needed a place where we had a little more privacy. After looking around, we found a staff sergeant who had a little apartment in back of his house and we decided to rent that. Since I had no car, I had to hitch a ride every day to the base. That apartment was one bedroom and a bath, plus a cubbyhole for a kitchen. It had only a hot plate to cook on, but we were alone together and it was okay for a while. I don't remember how long we stayed there, but it was not very long. Later we discovered a studio apartment with a stove and oven, and we decided to move there. All of those places had to be furnished since we had no furniture.

Money was very tight during that time in our life. We barely had enough to live on, much less any left over for anything else, but we didn't seem to mind because we had one another. While living at that apartment, I got into a poker game at the base on payday. I lost my whole paycheck and that was devastating! The guy that won my money came home with me and brought some whiskey and beer. He and I had a party. We were drinking what they call boilermakers—a glass filled with one-half whiskey and one-half beer. Margy didn't drink so all she could do was watch the spectacle while I got slobbering drunk. Margy told me later that she was a little frightened of the guy, but nothing happened. I was still woozy when I got up the next morning to go to the base. Margy said I was playing cards with the toast. As I look back on these irresponsible acts, I can't believe I was so stupid. Once again, I don't remember how long we lived there, but our next move was into a house with a couple we met. It was a real house with a yard and fruit trees. The new friends we made were Christians, and they begin to work on us to get us into church. They attended a little Foursquare church that was similar to the

Assembly of God church where my mom and dad attended. The pastor was a young man whose father was a leader in that movement. The first night we attended that church I went to the altar to receive Christ. I felt the Holy Spirit convicting me of my careless life. That was about the time my mom and dad visited us. It was Christmastime, and our landlord had given me a bottle of whiskey for Christmas. I poured it down the drain while everyone watched. I was really proud of myself. I even began to pay tithes to the church. I am sad to say that the change in me did not last very long.

The couple we lived with had some attitudes that really turned me off. For one thing, the girl got mad because my mom paid our part of the rent for that month and she thought they ought to help them out too. I thought that was very selfish of her, but I was not one to throw stones. Soon after Mom and Dad left, we moved into a small trailer in a mobile home park. It was not a mobile home—it was a travel trailer—and you could barely move around in it.

While living in the travel trailer, we met an Italian man and his German wife. The man's name was Salvador Santa Maria. I don't remember her name. We immediately clicked with that couple and began a real friendship with them. The German lady taught Margy how to cook spaghetti sauce the Italian way and we took turns making spaghetti for one another.

I'm not sure how long we lived there, but it wasn't long. I quit going to church when we left the other couple and moved into the travel trailer, but the pastor kept trying to get in touch with me. I believe he was sincerely interested in my salvation and I do believe he continued to pray for me.

Our next home was a little cottage in Leucadia, California, located right across the street from the ocean. The rent was only $50 per month. That was the nicest place we had ever rented. We could even hear the seals barking in the morning. Our landlord lived next door, or should I say landlady. Mrs. Largent, a very nice lady, was also the postmaster for that small town. She had a mentally challenged daughter that seemed to have an eye for me. I think she liked me. Mrs. Largent gave me work to do in her garden to help with paying the rent. As I recall, I was not very industrious at that time, so the extra job didn't last very long.

One incident that is still vivid in my mind was the morning I opened the door to get some milk left on the porch by the milkman—that was when you could have milk delivered to your door. I picked up the milk, and I caught the eye of Mrs. Largent's daughter. She was staring at me. It scared me so much that I dropped the milk and ran inside. She was quite harmless, but scary looking.

While we lived there, Margy got pregnant with our first child. By that time, we had borrowed enough money from Margy's mother to buy a 1949 Chevrolet sedan. We were really happy to have transportation at last. We paid $300 for the car. The time of Michael's birth will always remain a sensitive spot in my life. I remember taking Margy to the hospital on the base at Camp Pendleton. The doctor said we were early, but they would keep her there until the baby was born. I went back home after leaving her there, with every intention to clean the house and get ready for the baby and the new mother. I worked hard cleaning and preparing, but it didn't take long to finish the job.

There I sat idly waiting, which was a hard thing for me to do. I thought, I'll just go down to the local bar and kill some time with my friends. That was a bad idea. They kept offering me beer, but I was determined that I was not going to drink. Well, they went on and on until I gave in and drank a beer, then another, and another. I don't remember much about that night, but I know it was an all-night binge.

When I finally got a little sober, I went to the hospital and the baby had already been born. I felt like a bum. I still do when I

The Bridge Builder

think about it. I thank God for his forgiveness, but the memory has never left me. Even as I write this story, my eyes fill with tears of regret for letting my wife down. After Mike was born, we moved to base housing in Oceanside. We had a two-bedroom apartment that was convenient to the base. There we met Bud and Fran and became good friends with them. Bud was in the transportation area, and I was in heavy equipment.

I had become a little more responsible by that time and was not drinking as much. My friends, Joe and John Curtis, were back in our lives, and we would go to their girlfriends' house occasionally. They both were dating daughters of the mayor of Oceanside. They were out of the Marines and had good jobs. They soon married those girls. Joe and John were very generous, and at times they would slip us a $20 bill and tell us to go out somewhere. That really blessed us.

One incident is still vivid in my mind. We were visiting some friends in the apartment complex. The men played poker and I didn't know what the women did, but I knew Margy had gone to bed. I stayed until about midnight. We drank a few beers, but were not drunk. After breaking up the game, someone said, "Let's go down to the bar and get some more to drink." I said, "I can't. My wife has gone to bed." One of the guys said, "Come on, man. We'll be back in a little while, and she won't even know you were gone." They convinced me to go. After a few beers, we really felt our alcohol. We decided to go to Tijuana, Mexico. While we were in Tijuana, I met a guy who claimed to be a fellow Texan. By that time, I had so many drinks I didn't care. He asked us if he could get a ride to San Diego. Of course, we gave him a ride. We made it through the border all right, but when we were a mile or so past the checkpoint, the guy driving pulled over to the side of the road and ordered my friend out of the car. I couldn't believe he would act that way to my friend. He told him to put his hands on top of the car while he searched him. Well, he found that he had marijuana tied to his body inside his shirt. The guy driving then revealed that he was an undercover agent. We all ended up at the San Diego Police Department to give statements. In the meantime, it was getting pretty late in the morning. My wife wondered where I was. She called the base and talked to the captain. The captain said that I was on the hill with the equipment. My wife told him that she knew I wasn't, and that I had not come home all night. I was in trouble, but when I went to the base late that afternoon and told the captain what had happened, he let me off the hook.

As time went by, Margy became pregnant with our second child, Cindy. My mother and father came to visit us when Mike was about a year old. He was just beginning to walk. Margy went home with Mom and Dad and I moved back to the base. I'm not sure how long Margy was gone, but when it came time for the baby, she flew back to California to have her. We moved in with Bud and Fran since it wasn't too long before I was to be discharged from the Marines. Two families in a two-bedroom apartment made things a little tight, but we all seemed to get along pretty well.

I had made the rank of corporal, probably a year before I was due to be discharged, and just before leaving the corps, I was promoted to sergeant. About the time for me to be discharged, I came down with the Asiatic flu. They quarantined me for two weeks on the base. I was afraid that I would not be able to leave when my time was up.

Shortly after Cindy's birth, I was released from the Marines. I was discharged honorably and with a good conduct medal on November 10, 1957. Four long years in the United States Marines was over. Margy and I flew back to Houston with our two beautiful children to begin a new chapter in our lives.

CHAPTER 6
Salvation in Our Lives

MARGY AND I and our two kids moved in with my parents. They had just moved into a new custom-built home that was quite a step up from Kashmere Gardens. They had three bedrooms and two baths now. Dad still worked on the docks and made a good living for a laborer.

They had bought an extra lot next door to them, and they offered it to us to build a house on. We quickly accepted that most generous offer. Mom and Dad were good to us and helped us get a start in this new phase of our lives. I immediately went back to work on the docks. That seemed to be the best place for now.

After buying our first new car, things seemed to be going well, except I was still a selfish person. We got back in touch with our old friends from school, Conrad and Joyce Childress. Conrad was the best man at our wedding. The following New Year's Eve night, Margy and I went to their house for a small party. Of course there was plenty to drink, and as always I had no willpower to drink modestly. Once again, I got drunk. The worst part was that I had insisted on driving home in that condition. There was a big argument and I won. Only by the grace of God did I make it home with no accident. I can imagine how terrified my wife must have been. The next morning, I awoke early to go to work. Of course I had a hangover and did not feel well, but I was determined to go to work. Holidays always meant overtime and more money. After I had not driven very far from the house, I began to think about the night before. A strange feeling came over me, and my whole life began to flash before me like a picture. It reminded me of the old TV show, This Is Your Life. The Holy Spirit exposed what a selfish person I was. Every selfish choice began to flash before my eyes. Then I heard a voice calling to me, and it said, "Sonny, you are headed for destruction and you are taking your family with you. You must turn around now!" I had never had an experience like that before. It was like I was in the very presence of God. Immediately I turned the car around and headed back home. I told my mom what had happened and she said, "We're going to church tonight and you can go with us." That was the church where not only my mom and dad went, but my aunts and uncles and cousins and even Grandmother and Grandfather Jaynes went, and also Grandmother Walters. All of these folks had prayed for me for a long time. Never underestimate the power of prayer. That night, New Year's night, 1958, I went down to an old-fashioned altar in response to the evangelistic invitation. I emptied my life of all the old garbage and asked Jesus to come in and help me run my life. I don't recall the preacher's name or even the sermon topic, I just know God spoke and I responded. When I got up from the altar, I knew I was born again. I felt that I had a new start and was headed in the right direction for the first time in my life. After that night, my life began to take a turn. I quit drinking and using the gutter language that I grew up with and was so prevalent on the docks. As I drove to work two weeks later, the Holy Spirit spoke to me as I began to light up a cigarette. He said, "You don't need that anymore, you have me." I quit smoking that day.

As I wrote this story and remembered our experiences while living with my parents, I saw on the news that in California they were distributing condoms to anyone who requested them, from 12 to 18 years of age. It shocked me, because while living with my parents in 1958, Margy and I were trying to postpone having another child. Because I was too embarrassed to go to the local drugstore, I would purchase condoms from a local gas-station machine. They did not even have condoms on display at that time. What kind of a message does condom distribution send to the kids? "I shall," instead of "Thou shall not."

When I returned to work at the docks, they were installing a new seniority policy. That meant that the men with the most seniority would get the pick of the jobs. I believed that was definitely a step in the right direction, because before that, the foreman could hire their friends over men who had been there much longer. With the new policy, the man with the most time would get the pick of the jobs. The only problem was there were some young men who came to work before I returned from the military, and they were trying to stop veterans from receiving their military time. I began to pray that God would help us have our military time added to our seniority. I made a promise to God that, if He would help me, I would dedicate my job to Him, and I would use the advantage for service in the kingdom of God for His glory. I got together with several other men being deprived of their military time, and we went to the Veterans' Bureau of Reemployment Rights. We told them the story of what was happening in the International Longshoremen's Association (ILA). Those in authority immediately scheduled a meeting with the leaders of our union and ordered them to allow our military time to be used as part of our seniority. If they didn't, they would face a lawsuit by the government. God answered my prayer, and we received our seniority. I was determined to keep my promise to God.

After I got saved, I sure felt different on the inside. I no longer wanted to be a part of the world. My wife, who said she didn't want any part of that "Holy Roller" church, got saved the next night. Soon after getting saved, we moved into our new house next door to my mom and dad. It had three bedrooms and a bath. The kitchen and dining room were together with a nice living room. It was a real blessing to have our very own home. We also added a detached garage and we had a huge backyard for the kids to play in. We soon fenced it in and bought a collie dog. I had always wanted my own "Lassie."

Work on the docks was very hard labor, but I soon got used to it. Some of the cargo we loaded on ships was rice, fertilizer, flour, and cotton. Most of it was handled by hand. Usually, eight men worked in the hole of the ship doing the hard work. For the first few years, I usually worked there. Driving a forklift, or running a winch, or hooking up the cargo were considered key jobs. There was also the foreman and the flagman, the man who would flag the winch men as they lowered the cargo into the hole. One of the cargos that we handled was called carbon black, the materials used in tires to make them black. When we worked that cargo, I would come home so black that it took three baths to get the black off of me. Sometimes the black stayed around my eyes for days until it wore off. Like I said, those were the good old days.

I wanted a washing machine, so I began to work extra hours at night in order to pay for a new machine. How exciting it was to walk into the store and pay cash for that washing machine. God was good to us as we started our new life. My pastor, Brother Melvin Lake, was a good man. He spent a lot of time with me, and later I realized that he had discipled me. After a while, I was asked to teach the junior boys' Sunday school class, which I accepted willingly.

Margy and I were in church every time the doors opened: Sunday morning, Sunday night, and Wednesday night. I can't remember how long Brother Lake was my pastor, but I know it was not long, maybe two years. He wanted to bring an associate pastor on the payroll, but the board, which I was a part of, was totally against it. He then left the church and started another church not too far from us. I will never forget the heated meetings we had with some of the Assembly of God presbyters; one in particular came and apologized many years later for his unchristian attitude. Not long after his repentance, he went on to be with the Lord. Thank God for His mercy and forgiving spirit.

We began the process of hiring a new pastor. At first we approached Hilton Sutton, a tent evangelist with whom our family had become close friends. He had held revival meetings and had a tremendous anointing. He accepted the invitation, but then declined, saying that he had a check in his spirit. Later he started his own church for a while and became well known as an authority on Bible prophecy. We began looking for someone else. After praying to God to fill the position, we hired the Reverend John Giere, Jr. He was our pastor for approximately thirteen years. We immediately became close friends with that brother and his family. He had three children: Brenda, Karl, and Kendall.

About two years into my salvation experience we had a visiting minister, and he preached on receiving the baptism of the Holy Spirit. Although I was saved, I had never experienced that before. I'd had a bad experience in California at a tent meeting.

I went forward for prayer, and the woman evangelist pushed me down on the floor, claiming I was slain in the Spirit. A host of well-meaning people gathered around me shouting in tongues in my ear. It really scared me! While I was on the floor, I told God that if I ever got up from here I would never get in that position again. Here I was at a meeting where they were teaching the baptism of the Holy Spirit. I attended the meetings every night from Monday through Friday. At the end of each night, there would be a time of tarrying around the altar to receive the gift. The memory of that night in California would come back to me as all the well-meaning saints gathered around me trying to teach me how to speak in tongues. I would go home each night and search the Scriptures that I had written down. By Friday night, I had decided that God intended for me to be filled with the Holy Spirit. I felt the Bible was clear that it was a separate experience from salvation. When it came time to tarry, I remained in the pew. I went down on my knees, determined that I would not leave the church until God filled me with the Holy Spirit. I no more than knelt down when the Holy Spirit came in like a flood. I wept; I laughed, and then laughed again as wave after wave of genuine love flowed over me. I don't know how long I was there, but I did speak in a language I did not know. That experience has followed me many times again, as needed. The joy of the Lord continued to bless me. Often I would get jobs at the docks that I felt were a favor from God. The seniority I had received when returning from the military was a blessing.

    The one sport that I grew up with from childhood was fishing with my dad. Dad had purchased a beautiful red mahogany boat with a covered bow with portholes. The boat actually had room to sleep in the front of it. We often went fishing and water skiing. I had become quite a good skier. That boat was a far cry from the old skiffs we used to rent at San Leon on Galveston Bay.

One day when I came home from work a little early, I wanted to take Dad's boat to Lake Houston for some skiing. The lake was only 15 or 20 minutes from our house. I talked my brother, Johnny, who was only about 13 years old, into going with me and pulling me on the skies. We broke the lock on Dad's garage and borrowed his boat without permission. After a couple of hours of skiing, we headed home to face the music. I knew my dad would be mad, but I felt that if he had been there he would have let me use it. We were almost home when, as we turned into the street, a car hit the boat broadside. It knocked a big hole in the side of the boat. When Dad came home, we had to break the news to him. What I knew about Dad in the past brought fear into my heart. When we broke the news to my dad, he was mad, but he did not respond the way I expected. I actually saw the change in my dad, and Johnny and I were tremendously relieved. I swore never to take his boat again without permission. That incident prompted me to purchase my own boat. After a lot of shopping around, we found the boat I liked. The builder's name was Proskie. He built the most beautiful custom-made mahogany boat I had ever seen. Fiberglass was not popular back then. We also bought a brand new 50 hp. Johnson motor— the biggest motor they built at that time. The boat was colored a deep mahogany, with light cream-colored panels inside. I loved that boat very much and we fished and skied often.

My wife had always had a fear of water. She sometimes rode in the boat, but would never attempt skiing, and Mike and Cindy were too young, so I often went to the lake alone. One day after I'd had the boat for a while, I came home early from work. It was a beautiful day, so I decided to go to Lake Houston and see if there was someone there to pull me on the skis. I drove around the lake several times looking for someone to pull me on the skis. Then I pulled over to the shore and began polishing and admiring my boat. A young, very attractive girl, probably 21 or 22, approached my boat with a little boy about five or six years old. I heard a voice whisper in my ear (not God), "Why don't you ask the boy if he wants a ride." The girl was the one who answered, "He can't, but I can."

"Hop in," I said.

There I went, speeding around the lake with that attractive girl. Then I began to hear another voice whispering in my ear. I believe it was the voice of the Holy Spirit. He said, "Sonny, what do you think you're doing? You had better get that girl out of this boat."

I quickly pulled up to the shore and let her out without another word. I then got my truck and trailer and pulled my boat out of the water. About that time, my wife pulled up in her car. She said," What are you doing?"

"I just let my girlfriend out," I said. She didn't believe me then and I am not too sure she believes me even today. I learned a serious lesson that I have never forgotten. When the Bible says to "Flee youthful lust," it means get the heck out and away from any temptation. I went home that day and put my boat up for sale. A friend at the docks bought it right away. I didn't own another boat until many years later, while in the ministry, my dad gave me his old boat.

We lived in our new home for about four years. In the meantime, Mom and Dad sold their home and moved a few miles down the road to a new subdivision. At that time, Margy was pregnant with Brian Thomas, our youngest son. That was a time in my life when I struggled with the flesh. I worked hard and went to church three times a week. I had not developed a personal time of devotion, but depended instead on my church attendance. It seemed at that time there was very little talk about a personal relationship with God; everyone thought all you needed to do was go to church regularly. No one mentioned intimacy with God and time spent studying the word. If you went to church regularly and paid your tithes, you were all right. I began to grow cold. I had a lot of unanswered questions plaguing me all the time. One night I decided to quit fighting the flesh and just give in.

It was a Saturday and I had my check in my pocket. I decided to cash my check, get something to eat, and go out and get drunk. I called Margy and told her my plans. After cashing my check, I went to a local restaurant and began to have dinner and drink some beer. I had already given most of my check to the owner to keep for me so that I would not spend it all. That was a stupid thing to do, since I did not know the owner. As I sat there drinking, the Holy Spirit began to convict me. I could not shake the strong feeling that I was pulling a stupid stunt. After fighting the conviction for a while, I decided to go home. I went to the owner and got my money, then called Margy and told her I was coming home. When I got to my house, my pastor's car was in the driveway. I drove around for a while until his car was gone. They decided that if I saw the car I would not come in, so they hid the car. When I walked in the front door, there was my pastor looking at me with a puzzled look, like "why?" All he said was, "Would you like to talk?"

I said, "I guess so."

He followed me into the bedroom where I sat down on the side of the bed. He looked at me and said, "A righteous man may fall seven times, but he gets back up again. If I see your face at church tomorrow, I will know you decided to get back up." He then left the house. I wrestled all night with God, trying to decide what to do. After getting a little sleep, I woke up the next morning with this thought from the Bible: "Where can I go, for who has the words to eternal life?"

I looked back at my whole life and I thought to myself, I don't want to go back to what I was. I decided to get ready and go to church with my family. As I walked in the church door, the pastor was at the pulpit and he saw me coming in. He had a big grin on his face; it was as if God was smiling at me in a warm and welcoming way. I knew I was forgiven and was ready to move on to the next phase of my life.

Margy and I decided it was time to move. We sold our home and purchased two large lots down the street from where my mom and dad had moved. It was not far from where we lived. We picked out a beautiful white brick house that was on display at a local builder's place, and they started building on our lot. Meanwhile, we moved into a rental house across the street from where we lived. It was kind of shabby, but we thought it would be all right for a while. Brian was born there. We went through a difficult time with the builder. I guess that is par for the course. Plus, I was going through more struggles with my Christian life. Once again I began to look back at the world, struggling with a lot of temptations that faced me every day at the docks where I worked.

One night as I battled the enemy and my own flesh, I decided to go and talk to the pastor. It was late, but I knew I could catch him at his office. He was very approachable as a pastor. It is important in our walk with God that we have a relationship with our spiritual leader and others in the body of Christ in our church; it should be a place where we can be open and honest about our struggles. The Bible says, "…in the multitude of counselors there is safety" (Proverbs 11:14b). I don't mean we go to anybody or everybody until we find someone to agree with us, but we should go to our pastors and elders who we know will tell us the truth.

When I arrived at the church, sure enough, the pastor was in his study. I began to share with him all that I was going through, and he listened. Sometimes all we need is someone to listen to us. As I talked, I noticed two books lying on his desk. I picked them up and began to thumb through them. One was titled Deeper Experiences of Famous Christians. It was all about the famous men of God from Bible days through the 19th century. The other book was entitled In His Steps. I asked the pastor if I could borrow them, and he consented. I took them home that night and began to read In His Steps. It was a fictitious book, but a good story that gave me some comprehension about Scriptures that I was not sure I understood.

All night long, I would read a chapter and then weep with conviction. I seemed to be living with the characters in the book. I felt that I was learning what it meant to follow Jesus. I understood what the Lord meant when He said, "If anyone desires to come after Me, let him deny himself, and take up his cross, and follow Me" (Matt. 16:24). Jesus wanted me to deny my rights to myself and do what He wanted me to do. The cross was where my will and His intersected. In the garden, Jesus himself prayed, "…nevertheless not My will, but Yours, be done" (Luke 22:42b). The book highlighted the Scripture, "For to this you were called, because Christ also suffered for us, leaving us an example, that you should follow His steps." (1 Peter 2:21). If you are struggling with what it means to follow Jesus, pick up a copy of the book, In His Steps, and read it. The next couple of days after I read the book, I felt that God helped me purify my motives and gave me vision for the future. My heart was open for whatever God intended for the future. Shortly after reading these two books, one of my best Christian friends asked me if I would like to go to a family camp with him and his kids. I consented, not knowing that the trip would begin a new chapter in my life.

CHAPTER 7
New Challenges: Summer Camps

WHAT A GREAT time we had at Camp Pearl Wheat in Kerrville, Texas, the beautiful Hill Country. Pearl Wheat is the name of the lady who donated the campground to the Assembly of God. The camp was a great time of fun and games in the daytime with good old camp-meeting preaching at night. I never knew Christians could have so much fun. One night one of the speakers gave a prophecy from the pulpit. He didn't name any names, but I felt he spoke directly to me. "There is a young man in the congregation that God is calling to the ministry," he said. "This person will be used by God to encourage many to follow Jesus."

After the meeting one night, I was approached by Laurel Akers, the Assembly of God South Texas District Christ Ambassadors leader. He led one of the denomination's youth groups of ages twelve through thirty-five. He was a very good man who had helped many young men find direction for their lives. David

Roever was one of the young men he influenced. David became a well-known evangelist after he was wounded in the Vietnam War. His face had become disfigured very badly, but it did not hurt the anointing. Brother Akers asked me if I would meet with some other folks the next morning at the creek bank. He wanted to talk to us about youth camps, so I agreed. After our meeting the next morning, he asked me if I would be interested in working as a counselor in the camps. I had already sensed a pull by the Holy Spirit in that direction, so I said I would be interested. He then invited me to attend the next camp-workers seminar, and I agreed to be there. Little did I know how much that meeting would direct my life for years to come. I've learned over time that God gives us small steps to get us where He ultimately wants us to be. At the camp-workers meeting, I met two men who would have a definite impact on my life for years to come, Vic Schober and David Berkheimer. Both of these men were very anointed speakers. When they spoke, the Holy Spirit spoke deep into my heart.

The things that I had previously read in the books Pastor Giere had lent me began to challenge me to action. To work in youth camps would require me to leave work for one week without pay. When I volunteered for my first week in youth camps, I realized what it meant to take up my cross and follow Him.

I believe the first week of camp was during the summer of 1964. I was assigned to a cabin of about fifteen boys. As a counselor, my job was to be in charge of the cabin. I was to see that my boys cleaned their cabin and attended the meetings. I also had to see that they were in bed at the proper time. I had a wonderful time developing friendships with the boys. They were all of high school age and, for some reason, they seemed to like me. I think I had more fun than they did. I had never felt so accepted. I loved working in the camps and I became good friends with Laurel Akers, the director. Many of the boys came from homes where the dad was a pastor or evangelist. We called them P.K.s. The second year of summer camps, I volunteered for two weeks. During the second week, the guy who was to be the sheriff could not make it, and they asked me to take the job. I felt really honored that they would trust me with such a responsibility. The sheriff was close to the director of the camp. His job was to get the camp up on time in the morning. He was also overseer of cabin cleanup. I inspected the cabins every morning and awarded the best cabin. I also had to keep the camp on schedule, making sure that everyone was at the meetings on time, day and night. At night I had to be alert to any activities after curfew such as the girls raiding the boys' cabin or the boys raiding the girls' cabin. Of course it was all in fun, but it needed to be supervised. I enjoyed every minute of it.

I'll never forget that second week at the Friday night banquet. Laurel came to me and said that it was customary for the sheriff to pray over the meal at the banquet. Boy, was I scared! I had never prayed out loud publicly. I began to formulate in my mind how I would pray. When the time came and Laurel asked me to pray, I let loose with the long formal prayer I had worked on. After the prayer, Brother Akers leaned over to me and said, "I asked you to pray, not preach." I was embarrassed, but I learned a serious lesson. Don't pray long prayers at mealtime.

In 1966, the following year, God put it in my heart to volunteer to be the sheriff for the entire four weeks of summer camp. They were delighted to have someone they could depend on for the whole time. The four weeks of camp went by fast. I enjoyed being there and being of some use to the kingdom of God. Between camps I sometimes repaired screens and helped the camp maintenance man who lived in the house next to the campgrounds. I often dreamed of living in that house, so I could be close to the camp at all times. God had something else in mind. By that time, we had moved into our new home on White Thorn Street in the new subdivision where my mom and dad had moved previously. The subdivision was a farm that an old farmer had divided into lots. It had some good restrictions for investment protection. There were many large oak trees that gave plenty of shade on the lots. As a matter of fact, I began to build a tree house in one of the trees for my son, Michael. The power saw that I was using hit something and, not thinking, I grabbed the blade. Three of my fingers were almost cut off. I grabbed my fingers and rushed to the house.

My wife asked in alarm, "What happened?"

"I cut my fingers off," I replied, a bit in shock. After wrapping the fingers with a cloth to catch the blood, Margy rushed me to the hospital where, thankfully, they were able to save my fingers. Of course, that hindered my working performance for several weeks.

After a while, our church merged with the First Assembly of God in Spring, Texas, approximately twenty miles from where we lived. We had a good ways to go to church on Sundays. The church in Spring was located in front of a graveyard. After being in church for a while, we began to notice a young lady coming to the graveyard from time to time. One night the pastor called me. He said that young lady had him and his wife trapped in the church office with a pistol in her hand. I immediately hung up the phone, got my gun, and headed to Spring to free my pastor. By the time I got there, she had left, but the pastor did not know it. He seemed relieved when I opened the door and told him she was gone. Several times after that, she called the pastor with a deep demonic voice and cursed them with all kinds of foul language. She was definitely demon possessed.

One night as we were having service, she showed up and asked us if we could free her from demonic control. The pastor and I, with a couple of elders, began to pray for her to be delivered. God delivered her that night. The ladies in the audience said they saw the demons leave her. A foul smelling mist left her and went out of the church door. Margy and I tried to help her for a while. We bought her some clothes and took her home with us, but her deliverance was short-lived. I believe the demons came back seven times greater. We should have prayed for her to be filled with the Holy Spirit. I think we learned a serious lesson about deliverance. She called and harassed Margy and me for several days after that. Later we found out she received deliverance again and eventually married a minister—a good ending for a sad story. We never heard from her again.

Margy and I finally decided to sell our house and move to Spring, Texas. We wanted to be close to the church and to our pastor. It didn't take long to find a buyer. We moved into a two-bedroom apartment in Spring, just off I-45. In the meantime, the church purchased some property near the interstate and began to build a church. About that time, the ILA went on a long strike as they negotiated a new contract. It freed me to help build the new church. The strike was the longest in the history of the Houston ILA. Because we were out of work for so long, Margy and I spent all the money from the sale of our house to live on. We thought we were destined to live in that apartment for the duration, but God had other plans. While I stood on top of a ladder helping to build the church, Laurel Akers came and said, "You build God's house and He will build you a house." That turned out to be a prophetic statement. One day Margy and I decided to go looking for a house. We had no money for a down payment, but we knew God was true to His word.

We ended up in a subdivision just a few miles from the church, called North Forest. Margy had said she would like a four-bedroom house with a fireplace and two baths. I believe God read her thoughts. We found just the house; it met all her expectations, plus a two-car detached garage. We also found out that we could move in with no down payment and only a $50 deposit, which we could get back once the contract was final. Praise God!! We had a brand new home. What an awesome God! We had a brand new home and a new church building. Our strike was over at the docks and I was back at work.

We were in the new church building on Spring Cypress Road in Spring, Texas, when I met a newcomer to our church. His name was Ron Dryden. He had a beautiful singing voice and he had formerly played for the Dallas Cowboys. We became friends right away. At that time, my son, Mike, played football at Spring High School. They had a yearly football game between the teachers and the dads, and I asked Ron to play on our side. We had a blast playing flag football that night even though we lost, big time. Ron soon left First Assembly in Spring, and became the choir director for Faith Assembly of God located near the Northwest Mall in Houston, Texas, famous for its eternal flame on the top of the church steeple.

After a while in our new church, I became concerned about the direction of the church. It seemed that every effort to get folks interested in evangelism seemed to fail. I was Sunday school superintendent, youth leader, song leader, and Sunday school teacher. The work in our youth camps kept me fired up spiritually, but nothing seemed to fire up First Assembly of God, Spring, Texas. I tried to inspire the church with a plan to evangelize with Chick Tracts in our neighborhoods, but every effort was met with a lack of enthusiasm. I loved my pastor, but I began to criticize his sermons secretly in my heart. I began reading Watchman Nee's book on spiritual authority, and God dealt with me on my secret rebellion. One Sunday morning the Holy Spirit moved so strong in my heart that I had to get up before the whole church and confess my secret rebellion against the pastor. Of course I was forgiven and God changed my heart toward my pastor and the church. I have learned one thing in my years of experience: never leave the church because of your own discontent. Whatever there is between you and the pastor, always be kind enough to talk with him and not with everyone around you. Talking with others would be gossip. If you leave the church out of discontent, you will take that discontent with you wherever you go.

Several months went by and I was at peace with my pastor and the church where God had placed me. Then one morning as I woke up I seemed to hear the voice of the Holy Spirit say, "Sonny, go visit Happy Darnell's church." That was the church Ron Dryden attended. So Margy, myself and all our gang went to Faith Assembly of God for a most inspiring visit. The choir was much anointed. Ron sang with tears streaming down his cheeks, and his voice never cracked. That Sunday they took in 35 new members. I had never seen that many new members joining the church at one time. Our church usually never ran over 60 people. What a blessing! It was also a blessing to watch as the church filed by extending a right-hand of fellowship to these new members. As the service came to a close, I heard the voice of the Holy Spirit saying, "Sonny, this is where I want you for now."

We went home and notified the pastor at First Assembly that we were removing our letter and going to another church. Several people came to try and talk us out of leaving, including our very close friend the pastor, but to no avail because I felt confident that I had heard from God.

Our family seemed to fit right in at Faith Assembly of God. I joined my friend Ron in the choir and I loved every minute of it. Not long after we joined, the pastor asked me to take over as their youth pastor. That was an exciting time as God began to raise up youth pastors in churches across the land. I had been the youth pastor for several months when I decided to take our youth to a big Christ Ambassadors meeting in San Antonio. The conference lasted a couple of days and I thought it would be a great time for the kids. I believe Andre Crouch and his music were featured at that meeting. We packed up our things and headed for the big rally in San Antonio, Texas. What a great time we had! There was plenty of spiritual refreshment at that meeting. The sermons and the music were great, and everyone seemed to be blessed. The night before we left the meeting, I gave instructions for everyone to meet me at the van the next morning by no later than 8 a.m. They were to have all their belongings ready to leave. At 8 a.m. everyone was there, except two girls. It was misting rain at the time, so we went to their rooms to see if they were there. There was no sign of them. As 9 a.m. rolled around, they still were nowhere to be found. I began to drive up and down the rainy streets looking for them. Since these girls were only 16 years old, I began to be really concerned about them. It was a big city, and I could not imagine where they could be. As I drove down the streets in the misting rain, I spotted the two girls walking nonchalantly down the street. Needless to say, I was filled with righteous anger. I pulled up beside them and told them to get in the van. When they got in and sat down, I told them if they were my kids I would spank their butts good. When we got back home, one of them told her dad what I had said. He called the pastor to complain. The next day the pastor called me into his office and asked me if what the girls had said was true. I replied that I had said that to them and told him the whole story. He responded with, "Good for you. That's just what I would have done."

I knew then that the pastor was behind me 100%, and that is always reassuring. During the summer of 1972, I was committed to work in the camp for another four weeks. It was strictly a volunteer position and so was my job as a youth pastor. No salary was involved in either position. Now that was a different summer. Margy and I were scheduled to be in the camp in two weeks. At that time, we were going through some serious financial problems. We were broke. It looked like that would be a time to rely on faith. Because of my commitment to God, I settled in my mind that nothing would hold me back from going to camp. I remembered what I had read in the book, In His Steps, about what it meant to take up your cross and follow Him, and I remembered that the cross is where your will and God's intersect. As I began to leave church that Sunday morning, the pastor came up to me and told me to meet him in his office. One of the businessmen of the church was seated on his couch. The pastor handed me a check for $100. I looked at him totally shocked and said, "What am I supposed to do?" He said, "Take it and thank God." When I got to the car and showed my wife the check, she too was totally surprised. We had never received anything that we had not worked for, but God was preparing us for a lesson in faith and that was only the beginning. As we left church the following Sunday, one week before camp, the same businessman met us going out of the church door and shook our hands with another check. When I got to the car and opened it, we saw it was for $500. Back in the 70s, that was a lot of money. That came to $600 total, but that was not the end. On my way to work the next day, I was singing and praising God when once again I heard the voice of the Spirit. "Sonny, when was the last time you thanked your mother for all she has done for you?" I thought to myself, I don't remember ever thanking my mother for anything. At that time, my mom was completely backslidden and away from God. She was bitter toward the church and was drinking and gambling her life away. I responded to the Holy Spirit and told Him I would go by and see my mom if I had a break that day on my job. Sure enough, I got a two-hour break and I went to my mom's house. My grandmother came to the door when I rang the doorbell. She was living with my mom. She said that Mom had gone to the store and should be back any time, and I told her why I was there. She began to weep and stated that God had told her to help me out financially. She handed me a $100 bill. Wow! That made $700 so far. We had a good cry together and I started to leave when my mom showed up at the door. I told her why I was there and she began to weep. She said that she had received $300 more on her tax return than she expected and felt God had prompted her to give it to me. She wrote me a check for $300. That made $1,000 from the hand of God for provisions, but that still was not the end. The next day my wife received a phone call from Vic Schober, the camp director. He said that since Margy had made money in the snack shack, which was her job at the camp, they were going to pay her to run the snack shack. My wife and I not only learned a serious lesson on faith, but also on how God rewards the faithful.

The camp of 1972 was a very important time in the lives of our whole family. They changed my title from sheriff to head counselor. Margy was in charge of the snack shack. Mike, my son, and Cindy, my daughter, were lifeguards at the swimming pool. Junior high camps were held the first two weeks, and the last two weeks were high school camps. They were filled with fun and spiritual inspiration for all of us. But God used the third camp the most in my life.

CHAPTER 8
New Inspirations

CAMP IN THE summer of 1972 was the beginning of revival in my heart, in my family, and in a whole lot of young people at Camp Pearl Wheat. Vic Schober, the camp director and D-Cap for the South Texas district of Assembly of God, invited a group from California called "Agape Force" to come for a week of camp with the senior high group. The Agape Force, a newly formed group of radical young Christians fresh out of the late 60s and early 70s, was organized by Tony Salerno to train and equip young Christians to evangelize the world. Tony had been inspired by the life of General Booth of the Salvation Army. The group had formed a training program to develop Christian soldiers for the Army of Salvation. Their popularity quickly grew as they developed music and drama to reach the lost. Most of the workers came early to get things ready for camp. We were all waiting for the group to come, when we saw several Volkswagen vans pull up into the camp. What a motley looking crew filed out of those vehicles. Most of them had a definite hippie look, but you can't judge a book by its cover. Underneath the long hair and rugged looks were some of the most committed young Christians I had ever met. The whole week they were up before anyone else in the camp and out under the trees reading their Bibles. We assigned Agape Force members to be leaders in some of the cabins. The dorms were always the cleanest in the camp when lead by those members. The love of God emanated from that rugged group. Or may I say, from the God that they represented.

That week the camp speakers were Tony Salerno, the Agape Force director, and Chip Worthington from New Life Christian Center in Santa Rosa, California. Tony spoke on the broken heart of God and Chip spoke on spiritual authority. I had never heard any teaching up to that point that affected me like those two topics. Revival broke out at that camp of 250 students. My wife and I had quarters in the back of the camp office. Every day there would be a line of kids at the office, waiting to use the phone— they were calling home and confessing their rebellion to their parents. Many of those youth were called into the ministry and still serve God. God touched me deeper than He ever had.

One day Tony gave out a spiritual checkup sheet to the campers, and told them to find a shady place out under the tree and let God speak to them. I asked Tony to give me one, so I could see what the kids were doing. I took the sheet and found a shady spot and began to read and check off the areas where the Holy Spirit convicted me. When I finished, I went to Tony and told him that I didn't think I was saved. He told me the fact that I was able to see and to be honest about some areas of my life was an indication that I was saved.

After going over the checkup sheet, the Holy Spirit reminded me of a school bill that I had failed to pay at Southern Bible College. I added up what I thought I owed and tacked on 6% interest. It amounted to $75. I took the money to the school and told the lady at accounts receivable that I had come to pay my bill. She went to her files and came back and said she had no record of such a bill. I told her she might not have a record, but God did. I gave her the $75 and left.

One incident that happened during that camp made a permanent impression on my mind. Every morning at 6 a.m., we would have a prayer meeting in the tabernacle. One morning there were about 250 students praying. As I stood watching on the side of the hill, the Holy Spirit began to invade my mind. The sound of all the students praying sounded like a mighty rushing wind. I heard the Holy Spirit speak and He said, "Sonny, it's not enough for you to imitate Me; you must be Me."

It made me think about when Jesus left this earth; He left 12 men who would do the same thing He did while on earth. Isn't that the commission of the church?

Later on in the week of camp, a burly, bearded guy showed up. His name was Barry McGuire. I found out that he was a famous singer and actor on Broadway, and had played the leading role in the hit Broadway production of Hair—the first nude part on Broadway at that time. He had also written the controversial song, "The Eve of Destruction." But what really stood out was that this guy was full of the love of God. I liked him from the very beginning. I was told that an Agape Force person had witnessed to him on the streets in LA and that's when he got saved.

When the camp was over, I had experienced a week of genuine Holy Ghost revival. I hated to see the week come to an end, but that was not the end of Agape Force in Kerrville, Texas. They came back in 1973 and again in 1974.

That summer the camp moved to Silsbee, Texas, an area just east of Orange, Texas. It was not a good campground, but it proved to be an exciting time for me especially. The speaker that week spoke on the subject of the cost of discipleship. He had been influenced by a book written by Dietrich Bonhoeffer, a martyr from World War

II. It was a very hot and humid week. The temperatures were in the 90s, but the humidity made it feel like the 100s. One day I got into a wrestling match with a 15-year-old boy. I thought I was in pretty good shape from working on the docks, but that kid wore me out. I later found out that he was on the high school wrestling team. The Bible says "a haughty spirit goes before a fall," and I fell hard that day. I staggered back to my cabin that had no air conditioning, totally exhausted. I flopped on the bed and reached for my Bible beside the bed. I flipped it open and started reading, not expecting anything special, and I randomly opened the Bible to Isaiah chapter 58. As I read, some of the passages seemed to leap off the pages and go straight to the heart. I felt the Holy Spirit speaking to me the most beginning with verse 10. Here's what it said, "If you extend your soul to the hungry and satisfy the afflicted soul, then your light shall rise in the darkness, and your darkness shall be as the noonday. The Lord will guide you continually, and satisfy your soul in drought, and strengthen your bones; you shall be like a watered garden, and like a spring of water, whose waters do not fail. Those from among you shall build the old waste places; you shall raise up the foundation of many generations; and you shall be called the Repairer of the Breach, the Restorer of Streets to Dwell In" (Isaiah 58:10-12). The presence of God was so strong on me that I wept and praised God as I read those verses. Then I heard the voice of God just as I had heard it the day I got saved. He said, "Sonny, the last seven years have not been a sacrifice by you; it has been a blessing from me."

At that point, my mind raced over the last seven years and I realized what a blessing it had been for me to be able to work in the camp. It was more fun than I had ever had in my life. Then the Lord said, "Now I want you to build bridges for me." I was not sure what building bridges meant. All I had was the memory of a poem I once read called "The Bridge Builder," written by a man named Will Allen Dromgoole.

The Bridge Builder

An old man going a lone highway, Came, at the evening cold and gray, To a chasm vast and deep and wide.

Through which was flowing a sullen tide. The old man crossed in the twilight dim, The sullen stream had no fear for him; But he turned when safe on the other side And built a bridge to span the tide.

"Old man," said a fellow pilgrim near,

"You are wasting your strength with building here; Your journey will end with the ending day,

You never again will pass this way; You've crossed the chasm, deep and wide, Why build this bridge at evening tide?"

The builder lifted his old gray head;

"Good friend, in the path I have come," he said, "There followed after me to-day

A youth whose feet must pass this way. This chasm that has been as naught to me To that fair-haired youth may a pitfall be; He, too, must cross in the twilight dim;

Good friend, I am building this bridge for him!"

(Source: Father: An Anthology of Verse (EP Dutton & Company, 1931)

For some reason, I thought that poem had a message for me. I did not know exactly what, but I was content to wait for God's clear direction.

In 1973 I was invited to a Full Gospel Businessmen's breakfast. It was held on a Saturday morning. I wrestled with whether to go or not. Since the weekend at the docks was overtime and paid time and a half, it made the decision more difficult. I put the question to God in the form of a fleece. That was something I didn't usually do. But I said to God, "If you want me to go to this meeting, I will go if it's raining the morning of the event." Sure enough when I woke up Saturday morning, it was raining—and I mean really raining. So I got dressed and went to the meeting. There must have been 1,000 men there. It was held in a large hotel and I was seated at a table with a guy named Dick Babineaux. The speaker that morning was Pastor Conatser, from a large church in Dallas that met at the Bronco Bowl. He was a former Baptist minister who was filled with the Holy Spirit and joined the charismatic renewal, which was common during that movement. The question of whether or not it was a legitimate move will be answered further along in my story.

After the minister delivered his testimony, he invited everyone to come up front for prayer if they felt they needed it and I went forward. At that time in my life, my greatest weakness was my temper. As Brother Conatser approached me, I told him how sometimes I would lose my temper but would always seek forgiveness later.

With a straightforward look on his face, he said, "When you get too ashamed to ask for forgiveness, you will quit doing it."

The responsibility of self-control hit me squarely between the eyes. That was a lesson I needed to learn. At that meeting, I became friends with Brother Babineaux. He soon invited me to help him start a Full Gospel Businessmen's program at the hotel in the Houston International Airport. We had 25 men show up at our first meeting, and we soon grew to over 200 attendees. That's where I met John Osteen, a frequent speaker at our meetings. At that time, my son and daughter, Mike and Cindy, had become friends with some kids from West Columbia that they had met at youth camp. They organized a singing group and called themselves *The Big Thicket Singers*. I thought they sang very well, so we asked them to sing at our Full Gospel meeting. Some days later, John Osteen called Pastor Darnell and asked if he would release our family on a Sunday night to minister at his church. We happily went. The Big Thicket Singers gave a concert there and I shared testimony about what God was doing in our lives. My cousin, John, was on his board and, at that time, Osteen had only about 250 members. Later his church grew to over 10,000 members.

I had purchased a 1973 Oldsmobile Custom Cruiser; I believe partly due to the slight prosperity message that was prevalent at the Full Gospel Businessmen's meeting. Most of the men at these meetings were successful businessmen. No doubt they were godly men, but their measure of success seemed to be in how God had prospered their businesses. I never seemed to fit into that train of thought, especially since my heroes were men like George Mueller, Charles Finney, and some of the missionaries that left everything to go to the mission field.

I remember attending an area-wide conference they held. They had all the directors of the chapters line up and give a brief testimony. It was a statewide meeting so there were quite a few men there. Since I was considered a director, I had to give a testimony as well. I stood in line waiting my turn and listening to the other testimonies, which were mostly on how much God had prospered their business. I asked the Lord to help me with the words that best described what I did. As I approached the platform to share, God told me to tell them that I was in business for God and He supplied my needs by my labor at the Port of Houston.

Let me explain my work as a longshoreman, but first I will tell you why they called us longshoreman. Back years ago before they had large seaports, the ships with cargo would pull up to the docks to be unloaded. There would be a host of men gathered at the dock. The person in charge of the ship would yell out, "Hey, you, along the shore. You want to work?" That's where that name longshoreman came from. As a child, I remember going with my dad when payday came around. He would have cash to pay the men for their work. They had no union hall. All the men gathered at the foot of 75th Street, near where the ships turned around. At a young age, I was introduced to some very foul language. It seemed these men had a language of their own. I would see men gathered in huddles shooting dice, and there would also be poker games scattered around. Later on as I grew older, a large union hall was built were all the men would gather for hiring. Everybody showed up at that location when it was hiring time and the largest hiring time was at 6 a.m. in the morning. A large chalkboard listed the ships that were to be loaded or unloaded, how many gangs were needed, and how many men would make up each crew. We usually entered the hall around 6 a.m. and looked at the board to decide which foreman we would stalk for a job. The hall was marked off according to seniority. Whatever your seniority was, that's where you stood waiting for the foreman to offer you a job. You never directly asked a foreman for a job.

Cotton was the commodity that I usually wanted to handle. A cotton man had to be in good shape. Since that commodity was paid for by the piece, it was the highest paying job. The crew that worked cotton had to be well trained in the art of loading and storing the commodity. The men who handled cotton usually worked in teams of four, when possible. There would be a four-man team on the dock trucking the cotton with two-wheeled dollies. There would be eight men in the hole of the ship storing the cotton. A normal bale of cotton weighed around 550 pounds. The good crews could usually load over 200 bales per hour, and that usually averaged the men approximately $30-$35 per hour. The other job I usually sought was running the ship's cranes or winches. That was a very good job, because it took one man to run each crane or winch, and they had to hire at least two men. You could work two and one-half hours on and two and one-half hours off. If you got hired first, sometimes you could make a deal or you could work one-half day and be off the other half. I was pretty good at running the ship's crane since that was my job in the Marine Corps. When I first began to work on the docks, I had to work in the hole all the time and did not get to pick the key jobs. The best jobs were usually called key jobs. As I grew in seniority, the jobs got better and some of the time I had a fairly easy day. After a day's work, I would go by the hall at night to see if I could get a short overtime job. Any jobs before 8 a.m. in the morning or after 5 p.m. in the evening paid time and a half. A 10-hour day beginning at 7 a.m. and working to 6 p.m. would give two hours of overtime.

By 1974, Vic Schober had decided to start a church and he asked Margy and me to help him with that project. Herschel Rosser, who had worked with us in camps, also joined with Vic. Herschel had a very successful ministry with the Assembly of God called Chi Alpha, working with students on the large campus at the University of Houston. We left Faith Assembly of God, with God's blessing, to help start a church not far from where we lived in Spring, Texas.

Already God was speaking to me about full-time ministry. I was doing a lot of fasting and praying for direction in my life. I wanted to be in service for Jesus, but I had no formal training, just a sincere desire to be all I could be for His glory. I began to get out of debt, so I would be ready whenever God gave me direction. I had heard the voice of God while reading the Word, that I should owe no man anything. I sold my new Oldsmobile Custom Cruiser and bought a Volkswagen.

In the summer camp of 1974, Tony and the Agape Force were back ministering at the camp. I had been following their ministry since they came in 1972. Many times they had been to Houston, and Margy and I had put up several of the Agape Force team in our house. At that camp, Tony invited my wife and me out to California to visit with him at their headquarters. They offered to pay our airfare there and back. Since my wife and I had been nowhere after leaving the Marines, we quickly accepted. Tony arranged for us to fly to San Francisco where the Agape Force would pick us up and take us to their base in Sebastopol, about 50 miles from the San Francisco airport.

When we pulled into the Coffee Grounds, the name of the base, we were shocked to see such a beautiful place. The Agape Force had purchased the old Charles Shultz estate. It was like a country club on 28 acres of landscaped terrain, complete with fruit trees, a lake, a baseball field, a large swimming pool, tennis courts, a miniature golf course, and a four-hole golf course. There were several beautiful houses, and there was a large room next to the pool for classes. It was like a paradise to us. We had a good time with Tony and Kathy, along with some of their ministry leaders. We developed friendships with a lot of them. Tony took us to an Italian restaurant in Occidental, a small town about 12 miles west of the Coffee Grounds. It was some of the best Italian food I had ever eaten. California was beautiful and we had a great time; God is so good. While there, Tony offered me a scholarship to their discipleship school.

When I got back home, I had a lot to pray about. To go to the school would mean me being gone from home for eleven weeks. That's a long time, considering part of my preparation for ministry was to get out of debt. I had already sold my Oldsmobile and had been working on paying off any other debts I owed. The big thing would be our house note and utilities. However, the whole family was in favor of me going to the school, so I accepted Tony's offer and returned several weeks later to the Agape Force training school. That training was like going through the Marine Corps' boot camp all over again, minus the blood and meanness. Our director was Woody Shoemaker, who was an ex-Navy Seal. We were up and out at 6 a.m. for exercise and a mile run up what was called Heartbreak Hill. I thought I was in good shape until that trial. We would have breakfast of whatever was served, and then go to classes. Those classes had some of the best teachers I had ever been under. Some of those teachers were local. Two of them came from New Life Assembly of God in Santa Rosa, just a few miles away. Winkie Pratney, who later became a very close friend, was one of the keynote speakers. We also had Jim Argue and Chip Worthington, who had spoken at our youth camp in Kerrville. As another part of our training, we would go into town at night during the weekends to witness. The leaders would have us stand on the corner of the street where there was a signal light. When the light turned red, he ordered certain trainees to go out and preach to the people while they waited for the light to change. That was one of the hardest things I ever had to do. No one got saved, but it increased our boldness to witness. We had two outreaches during our training where we would go into town for a week to minister. We were each given five dollars, and we were required to return with those five dollars when our week was up. That would be a test of our faith that God would provide. At that point in my life it was more like insanity, but I would later learn better.

I ended my last week of training at one of their outreach bases in Denver, Colorado. It was run by a guy whose name I will withhold for good reason. He was someone who joined their group from one of our camps in Texas. That team had a coffeehouse on Colfax Street in downtown Denver. That was my first experience going door to door selling Agape Force records, one of the ministry's main sources of income. Some of the people seemed to be naturals at door-to-door sales, but I was not. I remember having a hard time as a teenager trying to earn money selling magazine subscriptions. It was very hard for me to come back to the ministry house without having sold one record. That was a big blow to my pride, when everyone else seemed to do so well. When the week finally ended, it was time to return home to my family. I really missed everyone and they all seemed very glad to see me. My son, Michael, had prepared a lobster dinner for the celebration. I had never had lobster before. That was Mike's beginning as a cook. What a joy to be home again. The old saying, "You never miss the water 'til the well runs dry," was true for me. I had a storehouse of teaching and revelation that God had planted in me during that training. God was doing the work, exposing the heart, and was about to teach me another lesson in humility.

When I approached my friends at church and at work with what I had learned it seemed like they shunned what I had to say. I was puzzled at some of the unresponsive reactions to what I considered revelation truths. On a Saturday night, I fell on my face before God and cried out to Him, "Lord, what is wrong with these people? Why won't they receive what I have to say?" What I heard God say was not what I wanted to hear. He said,

"Sonny, it is not the people; it's you. You have not shared the truth in love, but have shared in pride. What I have shared with you in these times was to draw you closer to me, not to make you someone special."

I began to weep in conviction as I realized what God was telling me, and it humbled me. I thought I was someone special just because I had training and had learned a lot of special things about God. I told the Lord I was sorry and if I had opportunity the next day at church I would confess to the congregation my lack of love. The next day we had a special speaker, and the topic of his message was how our intimacy with God was reflected by our relationships with one another. Talk about a double whammy; that was one. As I sat listening, I told the Lord that if I got a chance I would confess that sin as well to the whole congregation. I was a leader in the church and had been teaching discipleship in the college and career class, and I thought I would be totally rejected. The opposite was true. They all responded with love and understanding. I learned that God is more concerned with our honesty than with our superior religious attitude. The Bible says, "God resists the proud, but gives grace to the humble" (James 4:6). As the days went by, I could not keep my mind off of what was going on with the Agape Force. One day on the job, my dad said, "I'll be glad when you go where your mind is." That was like a prophetic statement to me. "Thanks, Dad. You just told me what God has been trying to tell me," I said.

I went home that evening and gathered my family together in the living room. I told him that God was calling me into service for Him. I told them it would mean giving up our home and all the luxury we were used to, but He would give us peace and joy in the Lord, and much more in return. I went around the room to everyone for a response. My wife said that she was with me in what God wanted. Mike, who had just graduated from high school, said he wanted to go with me. My daughter, who still had another year of high school, said she too wanted to go. Of course my son, Brian, was too young; he had to follow even though he may not have understood at the time. I notified Tony that we had decided to join the Army of Salvation, Agape Force.

At that time, we were pretty much out of debt except for our house. Tony told us that they were starting a ministry in Houston and that they would rent our house for whatever the mortgage payment was. We were all set. We bought our tickets and had $100 left over. Our pastor, Vic Schober, and all the congregation of our church gave us their blessings. The day we were to leave, the doorbell rang and it was Pastor Vic. He had $600 from an offering the church had taken up to give to us. Once again God provided with His faithfulness.

On our way to Sebastopol, California, we stopped off near Los Angeles to visit Ron and Linda Dryden, our friends from Faith Assembly of God, who had recently moved to California to work for a pharmaceutical company. We had a great time with our friends who later moved to Oklahoma to start a church.

CHAPTER 9
Life at Coffee Grounds

THE COFFEE GROUNDS used to belong to Charles Shultz, the Peanuts cartoonist. On the 28-acre property, there were two large houses and a two-story building that was used as a bookstore. The top floor had a little apartment that Winkie Pratney lived in. Margy and I had a room at the large house that was upstairs from the kitchen and dining rooms where everyone ate. Tony and Kathy had a suite down the hall from us. My daughter, Cindy, stayed at the girl's dorm, while Brian stayed in the men's dorm with Woody Shoemaker and the guys. As I have already mentioned, Woody was an ex-Navy seal and was in charge of the school. I had become part of the staff, and Margy had to go through the school along with Mike. Cindy, of course, had to enroll at the local high school to finish her education.

Winkie Pratney and his wife, Faeona, were from New Zealand. I loved to hear them talk with their funny accent. Winkie was one of the main teachers in the school. They lived on the grounds and would be in the states for six months, and then in New Zealand for six months. Winkie was an international speaker and traveled a lot. They had a little cottage amongst an apple orchard just to the north of Coffee Ground's compound. Margy and I lived in their little cottage when they were in New Zealand.

I enjoyed being part of such a powerful ministry. As the teams would return to the base, we would hear reports of how God was moving in the field of evangelism. On several occasions, I went on the school's outreaches since I was part of the school staff. On those outreaches, we became acquainted with a lot of nice people.

As we were going door to door in a predominantly Italian neighborhood, we met a very charismatic lady who invited us to come into her house. She was a breath of fresh air since we were cursed out at most of the houses. I had questioned the legitimacy of the charismatic movement. Since I had been involved with the Full Gospel Businessmen I had seen a lot of things that seemed hokey, but that lady was very nice and friendly. She wanted to show us something she taught in her Sunday school class. She had one of those flannel boards that you could stick things on. The flannel board had a figure of a spaceship or rocket on it. As she explained her lesson to us, my thoughts went to the question that had been on my mind for a long time. I heard the voice of God once again. He said, "Sonny you have been questioning the charismatic movement and whether it was legitimate or not. Well, it was! I poured out my Spirit to help bring together all the denominations, but there was some human-caused error. Power with Me is like that rocket ship on that flannel board. It comes in three stages. The first stage is grace, since you are saved by grace and not by works. The second stage is discipline, because you must discipline yourself for holiness. After that comes power. The error in that movement was they tried to jump from grace to power without discipline and holiness. There is too much division in my church." I felt that was a revelation from God, so I began to share the thought with several people and they, too, felt that I had heard from God.

One of the things that God was teaching me was that denominations were not God's original intention. I didn't think He was upset with them, but it was not His original intention. On the day of Pentecost, they were all in one accord. If you take the major emphasis out of every denomination, you get a picture of the whole. In 1 Corinthians 12:1-31, it says God put the body together as it pleased Him, not us. As I write this story, there is a major division in the body of Christ. Some ordain homosexuals that confess they are active in that lifestyle. That's not God's intent.

One of the outreaches that I was allowed to lead is very vivid in my mind. I led a team of students to Sunnyvale, California. Of course, we had our customary five dollars each with the order to bring that back after one week of outreach. Bonnie Wilkerson, the daughter of David Wilkerson, founder of Teen Challenge Ministries, was with me on the trip. Faithy Conn, the daughter of one of our major Bible teachers, was also with me. My wife was also part of my team, along with a guy named Roger Schurke, who had a degree in law as well as a pharmaceutical degree. That was quite a threat to a leader who did not even finish high school, but I had full confidence that God would help me lead properly.

When we arrived in Sunnyvale, we went to the park to pray. We needed God's direction. As we prayed for guidance, once again I thought I heard the still small voice of God say, "Sonny, what have you learned to do since you have been here?"

I said, "Go door to door." It seemed that I was getting instructions to go door to door and tell people that our team was there to minister to the young people on the streets at night. During the day, we wanted to serve the community by raking leaves, cleaning garages, painting, or cleaning house—free of charge. At night we went to San Jose to witness on the streets. With these instructions, we began our outreach. The people were so impressed with our team and the godly manner in which we worked that they gave us more money than we could have gotten had we asked. My wife and Roger went door to door to businesses. Can you imagine a middle-aged woman and a lawyer going to businesses asking to wash their windows or clean their toilets free of charge? They never washed a window or cleaned a toilet, but they received more donations than anyone on the team. I laughed, because I thought they gave them money just to get rid of them. When the week was up, we had received more money than anyone had ever received. We also learned a great lesson on faith.

One night after we had preached on the street corner downtown all day, I was preaching on the topic of being created in God's image and what that meant. A well-built Latino leaned up against a light pole listening to me preach. The guy looked as if he could be part of a street gang.

At first, his eyes seemed to emanate hatred, but as I preached, I saw his countenance literally change. When I finished, he walked over and asked if he could be part of our church. Of course we were not a part of a local church, so I asked if I could pray with him. He consented, and right there on that street corner he surrendered his life to Jesus. Our location that night amazed me. We were on the corner of First Street across from all the girlie shows—a very hard area. The streets roared with low riders circling the block. There was a lot of noise from the loud mufflers on cars. I went across the street to talk to the lady in the ticket booth at the girlie show. She told me she heard me preaching. That amazed me, because I don't know how she could have heard with all the street noise. God must have amplified what she needed to hear.

Another thing that stood out on that outreach was the time we attended an Episcopal church on a Sunday morning. They were very formal and unlike the church to which we were accustomed. At one point in the service, it seemed to get very quiet. Then out of the blue, one of the girls on our team began to sing "Amazing Grace," a cappella. It was a God thing, because you could sense the presence of God. After the service, people told us what a blessing it was and how they loved our team. The girl that sang was a young black girl, whose sister sang on the Agape Force music team called Candle.

After that outreach was over, we had so much money that I decided to reward everyone with a picnic in one of San Francisco's large parks. After the picnic, we went back to the base with much more money than what we left with. God had blessed us beyond our wildest expectations.

We were back at Coffee Grounds for just a short while when Tony told me they had purchased property in East Texas near Lindale. They said they were going to move everything there eventually. He informed me he was sending Woody to East Texas to oversee the construction. He then told me that I was going to be in charge of the school. What a shock! I had never done anything like that, and the weight of the responsibility for the students and that beautiful property would be on my shoulders. I felt a wave of fear come over me. I felt so inadequate for the job, and yet blessed that they would pick me to run the school.

That night about midnight I went to the office on top of the hill. I was restless and couldn't sleep; I begin to cry out to God for help. Once again I seemed to hear the voice in my spirit saying, "Sonny, I have called you there, and when I call you, I will equip you and give you the grace to do whatever you need." That was all I needed, just to be assured that God was going to be right there when I needed Him. I became the school director for several months. I had Steve Aubuchon as an excellent assistant. I had my wife and Kathy Fryer for the secretarial position. More than 60 students attended the first class when I was in charge. We had over 15 students from New Zealand. That would prove to be one of the most exciting experiences of my life. We had the regular host of teachers come in, and Winkie Pratney was the main teacher. Margy and I moved into the suite in the main house where Tony and Kathy had lived. They moved to Texas to be near the new construction. I became good friends with the pastor at New Life Christian Center. His name was Watson Argue; he later offered me a job working in his church, but I told him I was already committed to Agape Force.

God moved in a great way in that first class. He spoke to me in one of the chapels that we held just after the class arrived and we were gathered for orientation. God revealed to me that many of the students were there seeking their ministry. I told them that the Bible says, "… seek first the kingdom of God and His righteousness, and all these things shall be added to you" (Matt. 6:33). The kingdom of God is where the king reigns. If He reigns in our heart, then we are part of His kingdom. Our primary job is to do what the King says, and when we get that straight, He will give us whatever we need to serve Him.

On our first big outreach during that school, I took a large team to Sacramento, California, the state capital. What a great outreach that turned out to be. We slept and ate in some vacant rooms at a large apartment complex for one week at no charge. Our sleeping bags were our only furniture, but no one seemed to mind. The daytimes were filled with door-to-door adventures. We got permission to minister on the capitol lawn where people gathered to eat their lunch at noon and every day, we sang and preached the gospel. They even allowed us to hook up our PA system to their electrical outlets. Try doing that today! God granted us a favor. At night we had permits to preach in a large park where the Black Panthers used to hang out. The city officials tried to discourage us from going there because of the danger, but we were determined to minister in that park. As a result, we led two young black guys to the Lord. We ended up bringing them back to our base where they stayed for a short while.

I was blessed to be over the discipleship classes during that time. The schools lasted eleven weeks each. Between these eleven-week classes, I flew to Houston to work on the docks. I was trying to keep my seniority so that I could retire in four years, acting on Tony's advice. That proved to be a wise move for the future, and it became a real adventure in my life. I worked day and night, so I could acquire as many working hours as possible. My body would be at the docks, but my spirit was at the Agape Force campus. Time went by fast and soon Agape Force was ready to move the school to Texas. They moved me back to Houston to become part of the Houston team where they had a good outreach station started. Larry Powell was in charge of that team and we soon became friends.

Agape Force started a coffeehouse called The Station. It was an old abandoned church building, decorated inside to look like an old train station. Meetings were held every Friday and Saturday night. Singing, preaching, and testimonies were part of the program. Sometimes popular Christian groups were brought in. We had a great time at those meetings, and many were touched by the power of God. Late on Friday nights after the meetings, the Agape Force team gathered for prayer. After that, we would go witnessing on Westheimer Street in Houston where a lot of male prostitutes would hang out and party. What a great place to let your light shine.

One night we met a young man named Mark who was prostituting on the street. He was in his late teens and had been introduced to homosexuality by a schoolteacher in Massachusetts. He said he wanted to change his lifestyle, so Margy and I took him into our home. The young man was very intelligent, his mom and dad were divorced and his dad was some kind of professional businessman. After we moved Mark into our home, we made arrangements to have dinner with his father. We met at a restaurant on top of one of the tall buildings in downtown Houston. After that visit with his father, we concluded that his father did not seem to care what his son was doing. Mark lived with us for a short time while he finished high school. There were some incidents that took place that told me he needed more of a structured environment, so we sent him to Lindale, Texas, to the Agape Force School. He finished the school, but did not want to stay in the ministry. We were in touch with him a few times, but later discovered he was back into homosexuality and that was very disappointing to us.

Not long after we moved to Houston, Larry and Carol, who were in charge of the ministry, were called back to the Agape Force base in Lindale, Texas, and we were put in charge of the ministry in Houston. At that time, the ministry consisted of a coffeehouse and a women's ministry called the Mary House. We housed the men on staff next door to the coffeehouse. We had a house in the Fourth Ward run by Robert and Annie Duran; this is where the men lived who had been ministered to and had gotten saved. That wonderful couple became our lifelong friends.

Robert was an ex-drug addict who had been saved and delivered from drugs. He and his wife met in Agape Force and were married. Annie was the daughter of missionaries to China. Robert and Annie later became missionaries to Mexico. While they were there, they established a discipleship training school and planted 12 churches. They now live in Van, Texas, near Margy and me. Some of our staff worked in the juvenile department of the Houston Police Department. They liked our people working with troubled youth. While working in Houston, Margy and I met two other people who also became lifelong friends—Joe McShea and Ed Milewski. They were a couple of hitchhikers, moving through Houston. They came to the coffee house one night and discovered we had Bible studies on Wednesday nights. They started to attend on a regular basis. They said they had gotten saved, but had not yet settled down. After a few weeks, Joe came up to me one night and, with his Philly accent, said, "Brother Sonny, we're going to California to seek the Lord."

I replied, "Joe, you are just going to dope up again."

He countered with, "Oh no. We're going to seek the Lord."

About three or four weeks later, they showed up and Joe came to me and said, "Brother Jaynes, you were right. Can you get me some help?" He knew he needed structure and I made arrangements for him to go to our Agape Force training program. Ed went back on the road.

Ed later came back through Lindale to look up his buddy, Joe. He told his story for the Gates of Life newsletter:

> "Before I ever met Sonny Jaynes or the Gates of Life ministry, I had already asked the Lord to come into my life, but I didn't have any direction, or any spiritual guidance or leadership. I found myself reading the Bible, but then I'd still be partying too. I just didn't know how to break free from sinful habits.
>
> So I started traveling and that's when I met Sonny, in 1977, at an Agape Force meeting in Houston. The Lord

quickened my heart that this was a valid ministry that was really helping people, so I fellowshipped with them for a few months. But then went on my way.

About eight months later, I came to a point in my life where I knew I couldn't do it on my own. I'd tried to serve God my own way, but I couldn't do it.

At that point, the Lord brought me back to Texas and I knew that this would be my last chance to get my life straightened out, and that Jesus wanted me to stay in this ministry.

This was the spring of 1978, and the Lord began to set me free in areas where I never even knew I was in bondage—especially the area of rebellion. Once I saw I needed to submit my life to someone who was wiser than me and knew more about the Lord, that's when I began to be set free.

Bad habits like smoking cigarettes, drinking, and popping pills—they just went, as I submitted. As the rebellion went, then the bad habits went, and the Lord set me free day by day.

Now five years later, I can see that since I've been in the ministry, I've grown in so many ways. I've gotten married and have a child now, and the Lord just put a burden on my heart to help people. I've been on staff at Gates of Life for about 2 ½ years and I've learned a lot about myself and how to deal with problems of bitterness and rebellion, pride and anger, and selfishness—just the basic sins of mankind; always realizing that Jesus is the answer.

I just came to feel in my heart that it was time for me to go and multiply the ministry. I don't see the Gates of Life as a program; I see it as a family. I've seen men and women of God who really care, who really love.

I looked at their lives and I saw that they were really living for Jesus. I didn't see any sin in their lives; I saw humility. I saw honesty about them—not hiding, trying to kid themselves or anybody else. I saw a genuine love and I knew that God was with them and that God had sent them to help my life. I believe that when I began to trust the leadership, that's when my life was set free. I was delivered from rebellion when I saw that I was loved and that I needed to do what was right (Gates of Life, 1983)."

One young lady we met was Dinah Rundle. She had been in trouble with the law for various reasons that I won't discuss. She was a very attractive young lady. Her father was a very successful businessman, but he was not a Christian. We met on occasion for lunch and I gave him a book called Mere Christianity. Winkie had recommended that book for businessmen. Later on, her father became a Christian. Dinah lived with us for a short while, but later went to be with Keith Green, a popular Christian singer, in California.

We used different methods for ministering the Word of God on the streets. Often we would set up what we called the "gospel trailer" on a vacant lot in the Fourth Ward. We would have singing and testimonies and sometimes we showed the movie, The Cross and The Switchblade. It was a very effective tool for ministering. The vacant lot we used was across the street from a bar. Sometimes the people would stand outside and watch the service.

One thing that was very effective was when we held a mock funeral. We made a coffin out of wood like in the old Wild West movies. We would put a mirror inside the coffin so that when someone looked in they would see a reflection of their own face.

We then dressed up some guys in Grim Reaper clothes and had someone in front as a preacher. We walked down the street until we had people following the funeral procession. We led them to the vacant lot where we had the trailer set up. After a short message concerning the person in the coffin who ignored God and lived selfishly, we invited people to view the deceased. When they looked in the coffin, they saw themselves. It made some of the people very angry.

Several years after we moved to Lindale, we went by that site and noticed that the bar that was located across the street from our outreach had been torn down and a parking lot was in its place. Praise God! God revealed something to me one day while I traveled home from a day at the ministry office. I drove down the highway feeling pretty good about the ministry and about myself and the things that were accomplished by the ministry there in Houston. As I drove along, the Holy Spirit spoke, "Sonny, you see that man walking along the highway?"

I looked over and noticed a man walking and I said, "Yes."

He then said, "I love that man as much as I love you, and he doesn't even know me." Then He told me this powerful truth: "Sonny, I have always walked at the same pace. I'd never get in a hurry, so I want you to walk beside me so that you can hear me say, 'This is the way, walk ye in it.'" He reminded me of the Scripture in Isaiah 30:21. God wanted me to walk beside Him, not ahead of Him and not behind Him. Everything was going well at the Houston outreach station. One day out of the clear, some of the Agape Force leaders showed up and shut the whole ministry down. They took all of the equipment and closed all our houses down and moved the people to the base in Lindale, Texas. They had a house in Lindale open for our family, so we packed up our things and moved to Lindale.

Buddy Hicks, one of our teachers in the school and a good friend of Tony's, had moved out of a beautiful three-bedroom home in the Garden Valley Golf Resort area. It had a country club atmosphere. Margy and I settled in there for a while. Brian soon enrolled in Lindale Junior High School. He went out for football and made the team, first string. At that location, we met several men from the newly formed ministry called Calvary Commission. That ministry would soon grow into a worldwide outreach. They had moved into the house right next door. Barry McGuire, whom I had met in youth camps, lived on the other side of us. He too became a very good friend.

CHAPTER 10
The Beginning of Gates of Life

AFTER MOVING INTO that house, the Agape Force leaders approached us and said they needed someone to disciple young men with life-controlling problems. He asked us because he thought these men needed a good family atmosphere. I immediately felt connected to that idea. Margy and I turned our three-bedroom home into a ministry when we took in our first four men. Brian occupied one of the bedrooms and the four men occupied another room. Margy and I had the bedroom that would become our bedroom and office. We had two large walk-in closets that we also used as our prayer closets. We soon found that we needed those prayer closets more than an office. Sometimes when I had to make a difficult decision, I would go into my prayer closet and stay until the answer came. During that time, I continued to travel back and forth to Houston to work at the docks. Many times I would take some of the men with me to work. There was plenty of work at the port, and they always needed extra manpower.

Barry had an old Mercury Mirada; I think it was a 1967 model. I loved that old car and expressed to Barry how much I loved that car. One day there came a knock on my door and it was Barry with the keys to that car in his hands. He said the Lord told him to give me that car. I was blown away! That was a nice car and all it needed was a valve job. God is so good! That car had a hot engine. I've forgotten the horsepower rating it had, but I do know it was one of the hottest cars on the market at that time.

Barry introduced me to one of his old buddies who was also famous for playing the same role Barry played on Broadway, except he worked on the West Coast. That guy had an 80-foot yacht in Hawaii. He had just gotten saved and Barry asked me to spend time with him. We quickly became friends. His professional name was Red Shepherd. He had bushy red hair and wore white yacht clothes all the time. With Red's help, we did a valve job on that old Mercury. When we finished, that engine purred like a kitten.

One day, I decided to take it to Houston where I worked. I loaded the car with three other guys from my house and headed to Houston four hours away. We had to leave early in the morning in order to get to the union hall by 6 a.m. As we pulled into Houston, I fell asleep at the wheel just long enough to hit a telephone pole that seemed to jump out in front of me. I totaled the car. The Lord gives and the Lord takes away. Blessed be the name of the Lord. The only thing that was salvaged was the engine. I managed to sell it for $350.

The Agape Force purchased an old Mobile gas station on the corner of 110 and Interstate 20 in order to help us get a financial grip on the new ministry. We ran that for about one year. We sold gas and performed oil changes and grease jobs. People always remarked on how clean the restrooms were; we had the cleanest restrooms on the interstate. We also started an odd-jobs business. That proved the most lucrative since the gas station only lasted a short while because of the gas crunch of the late 70s.

We lived on the golf course only a short time. Soon we rented a large house in Van, Texas. The house had once belonged to an old, retired doctor. It had three bedrooms, and two of the bedrooms were very large with a bathroom for each. We moved bunk beds into one of the rooms so we could house at least six guys. At the front of the house, there was another large bedroom, as well as a smaller one. Margy and I had the large bedroom with a bath. Brian had the other one. We could have meetings in the living room between those two bedrooms. I am not sure how long we lived there, but I know it was not quite one year until we moved onto the ranch. Agape Force gave Margy and I a large trailer house at the back of the property. They made dormitories out of some of the rooms in the main office area. Since we had two large rooms, we tried to take girls in the beginning, but we soon found the quarters were too close for both girls and guys.

One incident stands out during our adventure in the beginning of Gates of Life. While at home visiting with my parents, my dad and I went to John Osteen's church for a Wednesday night service. By that time the Lakewood Church, John's ministry, had grown to over 10,000 members. After listening to John's sermon on faith, Dad and I went back to John's office to speak to him. He was leaving with his bodyguards and I asked him if he remembered me. He acknowledged that he did. I told him that I enjoyed his message, but I was wondering why I had guys sleeping on the floor because we had no beds for them. He replied, "Send me some information about your ministry."

When I got back home, I sent him a letter and some information. About two weeks later, we received a check for $1,000 from Lakewood Church. With that money, we bought the wood to make beds for the ministry. I designed beds with closets attached. One of our guys was a carpenter, so he built them. We used those beds until we closed the ministry many years later. They proved to be a great blessing.

Agape Force soon decided it was time for us to move again, and I went out searching for a place. As I drove through the back roads, I came upon a large brick house with a For Sale by Owner sign on it. I went to the door and asked if I could see the place. The owner was more than anxious to let me see it. The house was located on fifty acres of land. It was a split-bedroom design, with three large bedrooms on one end of the house and two baths. In between, there was a large living room and family room, a kitchen, and a dining room. On the other end was a large bedroom and a full bath, with a two-car attached garage. It was just right for our ministry. The seller was going through a divorce and was desperate to get out. He made me a fantastic deal that would be hard to turn down. At that time, the nation was going through a tough time economically. Interest rates were up to around 17%, so the deal he made was like a godsend for us.

I went to the leaders of Agape Force and asked for an advance on the $1,000 per month they had promised the ministry. I needed $5,000 to close the deal. They consented and we bought that large house and fifty acres of land for $125,000. The original owner carried a note for $50,000 at 4% interest, and the rest we had financed through Lindale State Bank. Gates of Life had its own location. No more moving at the whim of the leadership. They soon decided it was time to incorporate our ministry, which would separate us from Agape Force. That was another blessing from God that would later make us autonomous from Agape Force.

Just before moving into our new location, we met Ed and Betty Fugger, who soon became very good friends. They brought us a young lady that showed up at their church needing help. Ed and Betty were both well-educated Christians. Ed held a doctorate degree from Texas A&M as a reproduction physiologist, specializing in animal husbandry. He discovered the method for flushing embryos from a thoroughbred cow and transplanting them into another less valuable cow that would produce a thoroughbred animal. That discovery allowed them to jump forward in 25 years of genetic breeding.

After becoming good friends, we later made Ed and Betty part of our board of directors for the newly organized ministry, Gates of Life. One day we were discussing how to raise money for the ministry and finding useful work for the guys. Ed came up with an idea that we thought could bring in a lot of income.

The whole procedure of transplanting embryos was becoming very popular with cattle ranchers. Just before moving to our new location, Ed offered his expertise to form a company that would provide that service to ranchers. We went to the leaders and asked if we could use some of the land that Agape Force was not using. They consented, and after much prayer and organizing, we were ready to bring in our first customers. We were totally excited! Everything was in order. We had the approval of Tony and the elders, and we seemed to have the approval of God. We estimated that the business would bring in approximately $25,000 a month. Plus, it would provide much needed therapeutic work for the guys we were helping. We had 25 cows coming from Florida when we received a phone call from Tony saying they had decided not to allow us to use the ranch for cows. I was extremely disappointed. I don't know when I was ever so depressed. I moped around for several days, nursing the hurt and disappointment I felt. The ministry had let me down, and I felt God had forsaken me. After about three days of total despair, I woke up in the middle of the night and I stumbled into the kitchen area where a large parallel Bible lay on the table. It was a very thick Bible that had four translations in it. I told God that I needed answers to why it had happened. I opened the Bible and put my finger blindly on Habakkuk 3:17 and began to read. "Although the fig tree shall not blossom, neither shall fruit be in the vines, the labour of the olive shall fail, and the fields shall yield no meat; the flock shall be cut off from the fold, and there shall be no herd in the stalls; yet I will rejoice in the Lord. I will joy in the God of my salvation. The Lord God is my strength and he will make my feet like hinds' feet, and he will make me to walk upon mine high places" (Habakkuk 3:17-19a King James Version). I literally leaped from the chair and shouted in acclamation. God had answered me as directly as He ever had. Then that familiar voice said, "Sonny, if you had nothing, if you had no family, no ministry, and no business, would you still serve me?"

I answered out loud, "Yes, Lord."

I went back to bed and slept like a baby knowing that I had been through a serious test. That depression was gone and I was happy to be and to do whatever God wanted. We moved into our new house, which became the official location for Gates Of Life, Incorporated, for years to come. We started a new chapter in the life of Sonny and Margy Jaynes and family.

Photos

Sonny, age 3

Sonny Jaynes

Mom and Dad

Sonny, age 6

(l to r) Claude A. Jaynes, Stan Boykin (Margy's brother) and Tommy Jaynes my brother. Taken shortly after Tommy became a Christian and joined the Coast Guard Reserves.

Me and my brother Tommy about the time we were hunting with Mom and Dad. Tommy accidently fired the shot gun, ending our hunting trip with a bang. The picture was taken after they had taken us for new suits from Robert Hall's Suit Warehouse.

Sonny Jaynes

Sonny, age 16

Leonard and Martha Ravenhill celebrating his 85th birthday.

First concrete fence job God gave us. Spencer Cody (far left)

Grandpa Sonny and grandchildren on a rare ski trip to Taos, NM

Winkie and Fae Pratney having lunch with Margy and I in the Gates of Life Backyard.

Barry McGuire

The Bridge Builder

This is the crew for our ministry related business, Gateway Fence Company. Gateway was to become the financial support for Gates of Life, Inc. We soon grew to become one of the most prominent Fence Companies in the area.

Margy and I at our wedding.

One Proud Marine

This is the Agape Force when they arrived at our camp in 1972. The guy with the moustache is Tony Salerno, the founder.

From one of several trips Margy and I made to Washington Island WI with Dick and Eileen Harrison. They blessed us for over four years with much needed "getaways". The beautiful lady with that big fish is my wife.

A rare dinner engagement with Leonard and Martha Ravenhill, just prior to his passing.

Sonny Jaynes

(Top l to r) Brian Jaynes, Joshua Ward, Andrew Jaynes, Nicholas Jaynes, Zak Taylor, Mike Jaynes (second row l to r) Aaron Ward, Cindy Ward, Jennifer Jaynes, Whitney Ward, Judy Jaynes, Emily Jaynes, Christina Hicks, Tiffany Jaynes, Ashley Persing, Forest Persing (third row l to r) Zane Taylor, Tristan Hicks, Grandmother Jaynes, Grandpa Sonny, Jory Hicks (bottom row l to r) Tres Taylor, Michaela Hicks, Brian Christopher Jaynes, Ryan Ezekiel Jaynes Missing from photo, Lucy and Brighton Persing.

Brownsville Revival School of Ministry

CHAPTER 11
The Birth of Gateway Fence Company

LIFE AT THE Gates house was certainly not boring. Besides game times and the occasional movie, we would watch my son, Brian, play football for Lindale High School on Friday nights. Every Thanksgiving we had what we called the Turkey Bowl. Sometimes the school allowed us to use the high school stadium. After stuffing ourselves with plenty of turkey and dressing, we would get our team together and meet with a neighboring ministry to play football. The ministry we played was Calvary Commission, and we had lots of fun. My son, Brian, was our quarterback and coach. Even though I was old, or let's say older, I would play. I enjoyed it very much.

One day after playing on the football field that we made at the back of our property, I went to my closet where I had a desk, since that was the only place for an office. Lying on my desk was a note from my son, Brian. It read something like this, "Dad, please don't get mad at me, but I was wondering why you get onto me for talking to one of the guys in a hateful way when you do the same thing." That hit me pretty hard and I was convicted. I went to my son's room and told him I had received the note. I told him he was right, that I had no business to correct him for doing the same thing I did. I asked him to forgive me. Sometimes our greatest lessons are learned from our own children and, I might add, our wives.

It seemed since we couldn't have the animal business that we would continue with the odd-jobs business. Right after moving into our new location, we started helping a neighbor down the street from our new house who owned a fence company. His name was David Daffin. We sometimes jokingly called him Daffy Dave. That relationship would soon be the threshold to a totally new direction for Gates of Life.

David and I often had arguments over how much he paid the men that worked for him. After working for David for several months and having some squabbles over money, he came to me one day and said, "I think we ought to sever our relationship."

I thought about that very seriously, and the Lord reminded me that the Bible said in 2 Corinthians 5:18 that we were to be ministers of reconciliation. I told David that I did not think it was God's will for us to sever our relationship, but He intended for us to work out our differences. We agreed to meet once a week at his house or at mine for lunch. We agreed that we would not discuss business during lunch. The focus of our discussions would be on subjects unrelated to the business. That proved to be a very good idea and we soon grew closer in our relationship. We're still good friends as I am writing this book over 30 years later.

One day David came to me with a proposition that soon led us to owning a fence company. David had just acquired a contract with Trammell Crow, a real estate developer who had purchased approximately 8,000 acres of land that was once owned by a paper company. He wanted Dave to build 20 miles of barbed wire fence. David said if we would do the job and give him one half of the profit, he would turn the company over to us. After praying and receiving peace, we agreed. We bought a fence company. That move gave us a stable income for quite some time. We acquired a tractor and a post banger in the deal, and those items would allow us to build the fences rapidly. Soon after starting that job, we changed the name of the company to Gateway Fence Company, which seemed to be in keeping with our ministry name, Gates of Life. God gave me a vision that motivated me when work was slow. The vision was that we would become a popular company and that we would soon build all kinds of fences. Our motto became, "Fencing all of East Texas with all kinds of fence."

Around the end of 1984, when our work seemed to be very slow, I went out driving around to see if I could stir up business. I had not traveled far from the house where our business was located when, just off Highway 110, I spotted a large construction site and decided to stop. After locating the superintendent, I asked him if there would be any fences on the site. He told me that there would be lots of fence. I asked him if they would allow me to bid on the job. He said he would check with his boss and get back with me. It wasn't long before he called me back and told me that Mr. Williams, the owner, wanted a concrete fence around the perimeter of the property. I had never heard of a concrete fence, but I did not let him know that fact. I told him I would work a bid for him. I had plenty of time, because it would be quite some time before they would be ready. I began to scramble around trying to find out about concrete fences. I soon learned that they had some concrete fences in Las Colinas, just outside of Dallas, made by a company in Houston. I also learned there was a plant that made concrete fences around the corner from my mom and dad. It seemed as if God was helping me put the thing together. I made a visit to Mom and Dad's to check on that fence. I acquired some very good brochures giving information about the fence, and some good pictures. I went back home and began to formulate a plan. In the meantime, I did not stop looking for other companies that had that type of fence. I soon found out there was a company near Los Angeles, California, that also made concrete fences.

After talking to the owners over the phone and getting prices, I decided they had a better product. I cut out the pictures that I got from the brochures and wrote a letter to Mr. Williams with the pictures enclosed. As I put the letter in the mailbox on a Saturday, I prayed for God's favor. Monday evening, I received a phone call from Mr. Williams' office. They wanted to set up a meeting to discuss the fence. Once again I felt God was coming through with His favor. We set up a date to meet with Mr. Williams and his wife at a restaurant on Interstate 20.

As we sat down for breakfast at the restaurant with Mr. Williams and his wife, I was filled with excitement and expectation. Mr. Williams was a very wealthy construction owner. He built skyscrapers in Dallas and New York. I found out that he had purchased some property in Dallas where he planned to build the tallest building in the world. He had just sold his business in New York for over $250 million. The ranch he was putting the fence around was over 1700 acres. It was to be a show ranch for horses and cattle. For the first hour of our conversation, Mr. Williams and his wife asked me all kinds of questions about the ministry of Gates of Life. When we finally got down to discussing the fence, he asked me if I could fly out with him to look at the product. He had a private jet and we could go to California and back in a day. Of course I agreed, holding back the sheer excitement of flying in someone's private jet. We made a date to go to California in two weeks. About the time to go, Mr. Williams called to cancel our engagement. He asked me to have the California company send a section of the fence in the mail at his expense. Of course I agreed, but I was truly disappointed that I would not get to ride in his jet. Soon after I ordered the fence section, it arrived. We set the section of fence in our front yard, and then called Mr. Williams to set up a time for him to see the fence. We prepared a great spread of sandwiches and refreshments for Mr. Williams. My wife arranged everything very nicely for his visit to our house. Soon he arrived in his Rolls-Royce Silver Cloud, driving into my driveway of sand. When he entered the house, he went straight to the closed-in patio where we had a ping pong table. He made a comment that he used to play ping pong. We offered him lunch, but he declined and said, "Let's look at the fence."

Mr. Williams was impressed with the fence and asked me to work up a bid. He said that he would need about five miles of the fence. That's a lot of concrete! I began to figure out all the expense and what it would take to install the fence. We called the California company for prices on the fence, plus shipping costs. The total came to $13.50 per linear foot. That amounted to over $350,000. That would be the biggest job we would ever have. Once again, I felt God's favor.

After submitting the bid, time went by and we did not hear from Mr. Williams. I had my son, Brian, draw up a contract. I had scheduled a conference in Austin, Texas, with Bill Gothard Ministries. On the way there, Brian and I planned to stop by Mr. Williams' office in Dallas. His office was on the top floor of one of his glass skyscrapers. As we stepped out of the elevator, we instantly entered his office. We asked for Mr. Williams, but his receptionist said that he was not in yet. We met with the superintendent of his company who told us that Mr. Williams would be in shortly and we should wait just outside the elevator. It wasn't long before Mr. Williams stepped out of the elevator. He immediately recognized us and we were invited into his office. He told us he was considering installing the fence with his crew and buying the materials from us, giving us a good markup. I informed him that we wanted to install the fence, because it would give us the notoriety our company needed. He then told us to leave the contract and he would think about it. When Brian and I arrived at the motel in Austin, we received a call from my wife saying Mr. Williams had signed the contract for five miles of concrete fence. Once again I thanked God for His answer to my prayer. That one job proved to be a blessing for years to come. It provided finances and stability to our business and ministry.

One day we received a notice from the IRS that they would be auditing our ministry. We were not sure what that meant and, like everyone else, we were a little afraid of the IRS. Our primary concern was that we might earn too much money to qualify as a nonprofit organization. We waited carefully for the day when they would come. They soon arrived, or I might say he did, for it was only one person. He was very nice to us and we treated him with respect and the best of southern hospitality. For three days, he wrestled with our unorganized books. Although our books were a mess, I think he realized it was unintentional. Before he left, he gave us a clean bill of health and showed us how to keep our books. We also found out while he was there that he was a Jew by birth, and that his daughter had become a born-again Christian.

Just before we got the big job with Mr. Williams, we were struggling with our house payment. Things got so tight that I decided to refinance our house to get the payments lower and more manageable. We also needed about $8,000 for insurance.

All of that put pressure on me to make the decision to refinance. That proved to be the wrong move. I think that I only lowered our payment a couple of hundred dollars. Margy and I were scheduled to go to California for an Agape Force conference, so I quickly signed all the papers and got the ball rolling. I wish I had waited until we got home. We had no more than arrived at California when my secretary called and said, "Melody Green of Last Days Ministry called and said they were sending us a check for $8,000 and a pledge of $500 a month in continued support."

We were very excited and I was very sorry I had not trusted God. That mistake haunted me for a long time to come. The Bible says, "Trust in the Lord with all your heart, and lean not on your own understanding; in all your ways acknowledge Him, and He will direct your paths" (Proverbs 3: 5-6). Around that time, we had our first adventure traveling on the road with our newly formed singing group called Morning Song. Our first tour consisted of Burt Forney, Charlie Morgan, Ken Dustin, and my son, Brian. Charlie was a gifted singer and piano player, and he helped get the group going. Margy became the one who organized our first tour. She got on the phone and called around for bookings. She soon had a tour put together. The tour started with a youth camp in Kerrville, Texas, where I would be the main speaker and Morning Song would provide the music. Margy's cousin's husband lent us his motorhome for traveling. We bought a PA system that was small enough to pack into our motorhome.

After a week in Kerrville, we headed for Houma, Louisiana. We had a service there with Laurel Akers' brother, Noel. We then headed for Florida. On the way to Florida, we had a flat tire. None of us knew what to do with a flat tire on that big motorhome. We sat down on the side of the road, puzzled at what we should do.

A family in another motorhome stopped and helped us get our flat tire changed. We instantly became good friends. We told them that we were on our way to Florida, but we would eventually end up in Rockford, Illinois. That's where those folks were from. We made a date for them to visit us at our service in Rockford. Once again, we could see the hand of the Lord arrange that meeting.

We had an engagement in Gainesville, Florida, at a Maranatha conference. We were only there for a short time, but received the largest contribution of the whole trip. After arriving in Florida, we met up with an old friend from our Marine Corps days, Fran, who was divorced from her husband, Bud. We had a great visit with those folks and their children. We were able to share testimonies that I believed touch their hearts. A couple of days later, we headed for Georgia where we had a service in an Assembly of God church. Then we went up to Tennessee, where we had another service at Jimmy Swaggart's cousin's church. After Tennessee, we headed for Rockford, Illinois. We met with a college and career group in a large Assembly of God church. About 250 young people attended that meeting. It was a special time, since we were to meet the couple who helped us with our flat tire in Louisiana. After the service, we went to their home and met with their whole family. We sang for them and shared testimonies. What a great time in the Lord we had. From Rockford, we traveled to Carbondale where we met the Rooker family. They had heard about our ministry and wrote asking us to visit if we were in the area. The Rooker family moved to Texas to become part of our ministry soon after we met. That would be a relationship that would last for years to come. Rhonda became our secretary and David worked in the fence company. David and Rhonda had three boys; their names were James, Michael, and Robbie. David was a hard worker and soon adapted to building fences.

He also was an accomplished musician, and played the piano and sang with our singing group.

After a couple of years, they moved on in a different direction, but they remained faithful to Community Christian Fellowship for years to come. David took charge of The Scroll Christian Discount Store, a not-for-profit Christian bookstore, and was quite successful.

Morning Song's first tour was such a blessing that we thought Margy should plan another trip for us. We decided to go to the West Coast next. Our new group was made up of Charlie Morgan, Burt Forney, and Cathy Dykes, a local friend. We felt that a slightly smaller group would be better for traveling, and less expensive. The new group began to practice and get ready, while Margy put the trip together. Margy was a very important part of our ministry. She was a true mom to the guys, and a blessing to me as my wife. I could never have accomplished this without her. She was a good example of unconditional love. As the time approached to go on our tour, something came up that put a cramp on our plans. The devil loves to throw us a curve once in a while to discourage us. One thing I have learned through all the years of ministry, God loves to use the devil's tricks to test and prove us. When we go into a difficult time, we need to stop and ask God, "What are you trying to teach me through this trial?" Sometimes our first response is to throw up our hands and quit. That's just what the devil wants. As the time approached to go on our trip, I sent Charlie to town with my van and $1,000 in cash to deposit in the bank for the trip. Charlie never came back. He not only took our transportation, but he also took our money for the trip.

We had some serious praying to do since the trip was already planned. We had no van, no money, and no piano player. We were not about to give up.

Cathy Dykes had a little sister who was just a teenager, maybe 16 years old, who could play the piano very well. We had her practice our songs and we recorded her music on a cassette tape to use as background. The singers adapted well to that plan. We also drafted our youngest guy, John Davis, as one of the singers. He had a very good voice and learned the songs quickly. I then went out and shopped for a van. I found a used luxury van on a car lot in town and purchased it at a reasonable price. It was a converted fifteen-passenger van. It had two captain's chairs and a couch, with plenty of cargo space. That van lasted a long time. We were ready to go, and the devil was defeated one more time. Our trip actually began in Mineola, Texas, at a Baptist church whose pastor was the brother of our family doctor. From there we traveled west to Midland, Texas. We had a service at the First Assembly of God in that town. Then we moved on to El Paso, Texas, where we ventured into Juarez, Mexico. We spent a short time there, mostly as tourists. From there we traveled straight to Napa Valley, California, where we held a service at the First Assembly of God. We had met the pastor in Kerrville while working in camps. After a very moving service in Napa Valley, we went on to be with my good friends, Gail and Woody Shoemaker, former director of the discipleship training school for Agape Force. They were actively growing a family and pastoring the Cayuga Christian Fellowship in Cayuga, California. It was good to visit with Gail and Woody. He was a no-nonsense Christian, and I held him in high esteem.

From Cayuga we went to Glendale, California. There we met Charlie Morgan's mother, as well as his grandmother, an active member of the Salvation Army. Charlie's grandmother had worked with Commissioner Samuel Logan Brengle, the author of a whole series of books on holiness. We hit it off right away since he was one of my spiritual heroes, along with General

Booth. We also met Charlie's sister, Kathy. We later became close friends when she moved to Texas.

After returning home from the trip, we learned that Charlie had been caught and sentenced to one year in prison at the unit in Sugar Land, Texas. The van had been totaled and the money spent. Margy and I surprised him with a visit while he was in prison, and after his year in prison, he was paroled back to us at the ministry. As restitution, Charlie converted our two-car garage into a private office for me. He also made us a handcrafted table to seat twelve people. That table served us for many years.

About that time, we became acquainted with Brother Leonard Ravenhill, who moved to the area to teach in the Agape Force discipleship program. He began holding prayer meetings at the Brown's house, and then moved to the campus at Last Days. Prayer meetings were held every Friday night, and I would take some of the guys to those meetings. Later on, Brother Leonard moved the meetings to his house and invited just a few men and fortunately I was one of them. It was not long before we became good friends with Brother Leonard. I sometimes drove him to local meetings where he would preach. Several of the guys would usually go with us. Often Brother Leonard called my house if he did not hear from me. He always asked my wife if "The Bishop" was there. Can you imagine Brother Leonard Ravenhill calling me "The Bishop?" He was a wonderful person to be around, always full of dry humor. What an honor to have such a great evangelist and prophet as a friend. Later on, I was privileged to be a pallbearer at his funeral.

Meanwhile, the concrete fence contract did just what I thought it would do. It gave us tremendous notoriety. We put a large sign up on Interstate 20 so people could see that our company was building that fence. We began to get lots of phone calls inquiring about the fence. It was the talk of all the truckers traveling I-20.

People began to contact us to purchase fences. Pierre, the owner of the company in California, came down to Texas to discuss possibilities of establishing a plant here in Tyler. He soon purchased some property at the East Texas industrial site, just north of Tyler. Pierre's brother, Dan, came down from California to set up the plant. Those two brothers were Dutch men that lived in South Africa. They were ex-mercenaries and tough as nails. They made the fence and we became their installers. That worked out very well for us, and we began to get jobs all around the area. Dan soon decided we were making more money than he was, so he decided to get his own installers. That became a disaster for him. They messed up a job, had a lawsuit filed against them, and had to declare bankruptcy. We found ourselves with lots of jobs and nobody to make the fence. I went to talk to Dan to see what we could work out. Once again, God came through with a blessing beyond words to describe. Dan offered to turn the plant over to us for no charge at all—the building, the molds, the cement mixers, and the forklift. He also offered to train my guys to make the materials. Thus began another adventure for Gateway Fence Company and Gates of Life. We were in business making three-rail fence materials; it was like a gift straight from God. We had four guys working at the plant making three-rail fence materials, and Dan stayed around to help supervise the men. I believe our men really impressed Dan. I even talked Dan into going to our church one night. I found out that he and his brothers were once Spirit-filled believers and belonged to the Apostolic Church in South Africa.

We also ventured into making custom ornamental-iron fences and fancy gates with automatic gate openers. I would draw out and design entryways. It was all part of the vision I had when we first acquired the fence company. The business soon became our only source of income. It also provided work for the men and the ability to learn a useful trade. They learned to install fence and to weld, and since we had about five trucks, they also learned auto mechanics. I don't believe the cattle business would have been as good for the ministry as building fence was. God always makes a way when there seems to be no way. We just need to learn to trust Him. I had never built a fence in my life. God was the one who put the whole thing together.

As our company began to grow, we purchased welding equipment and began to do a lot of welding. At that time I had been teaching a Bible course at Calvary Commission. That ministry had begun to develop a home for orphans in Mexico. They also had a Bible school in the same location. While I was there teaching I noticed there was no playground equipment for the children to play on, and there were no fences. I volunteered to bring our crew to Mexico. We loaded all of our welding equipment in our truck and I took several men with me to build a fence and playground equipment out of oil-field pipe. We were blessed to be able to do that for the orphanage. That home was named after Keith Green's children that died in the plane crash at Last Days Ministry. I am sure those playgrounds still exist.

CHAPTER 12
Continuing the Journey: Changed Lives

THE JOURNEY HAD been very exciting. God moved in my life much or more than the men He sent me. Exciting does not always mean fun, however, for God had done a deep surgical work on my heart. The Bible says, "Iron sharpens iron, so a man sharpens the countenance of his friend" (Prov.27:17).

Because I had encountered so many problems that I had no experience in dealing with, I began to study about counseling through men who were educated on the subject. I read books such as The Christian Counselor's Manual and Competent to Counsel, both by Jay Adams. One book that really helped me to understand my own problems, as well as those of the men I was working with, was a book entitled Reality Therapy by William Glasser. These studies allowed things in my life to surface. God exposed my own insecurities and failures in raising my children. Those spiritual surgeries helped me deal with not only the men, but also myself. I learned that while many of the dysfunctions in our own lives have a lot of influence on us, they are not the causes of our behavior. My reaction to problems was learned by observing the way my parents acted. As I observed the life of Jesus, I began to have a deepening desire to be like Him. My daughter was the only one around to see some of the changes taking place in me. My two sons were off at that time pursuing their own directions in life. My son, Brian, moved to Dallas shortly after we acquired the fence contract. He got into the automobile business, along with his brother Michael. Both were very good in that business.

Life at Gates of Life was not just work and church. We also led the men on several outreach projects in Houston and in Tyler, Texas For approximately 10 years, I conducted a Friday night prayer meeting at the Community Christian Fellowship Church where I was an elder. We had an open mike where different people could come up and pray or quote Scripture. Our prayers were focused mostly on revival in our church and our country. After the prayer meeting, we invited the folks to join us at the Downtown Tyler Square where kids hung out to party. For a long time, we went there and witnessed to the kids that were smoking their dope and making out. We became discouraged when most of the time the kids said they were saved, but their lives certainly did not show it. We decided to go to the square and just worship and pray and claim the territory for God. After several months, we noticed that the teenagers were not there anymore. Even until this day, they don't hang out there. God does answer prayer.

We also made several trips to Houston and stayed at the Salvation Army, where one of the guys we met at the coffeehouse in Houston worked as a counselor. We stayed at the Salvation Army facility and ministered there in the daytime. At night we went to the streets in the Westheimer area to pass out tracts and to witness. We ministered on Westheimer in front of a teen party place where a lot of punk rockers were doing what they called slam dancing. I could not believe parents allowed their kids to attend that ungodly place, but they were dropping their kids off to participate in the wild party. We began to pray that God would shut that place down. We prayed loudly and with authority. A few months later, we went by that place and it was all boarded up. We praised God for answering our prayer.

Life at the Gates house was very challenging with so many men living together in two rooms. My wife always said, "Living in the house with eight to ten men will surely test your Christianity." Often, relational conflicts developed between the men of varying backgrounds. The only way I succeeded in bringing peace was to hold chapel and minister to the men from God's Word, especially the part in Matthew 7:3-5 when Jesus talked about first removing the plank in your own eye before looking at the spec in your brother's eye. I explained that often the plank in your eye is your overreaction to the spec in your brother's eye.

Usually after a brief teaching session, we would have a foot washing-service, and then we'd take communion. Washing someone's feet is very humbling, and having your feet washed is even more humbling. Frequently the Holy Spirit brought a strong conviction that resulted in hugging and forgiving and restoring peace.

JW

A story recently surfaced when we heard from a young man we had not heard from in over thirty years. I will call him JW for his protection. He told us that he had been trying to get hold of us for a long time. I received a phone call from one of the men who used to work for me and he told me JW had contacted him looking for our phone number.

Over thirty years ago we met JW, a kid we ministered to in the LTI reform school in Louisiana. We felt attached to him, so we took him home with us to try and help him. He sent us his story by e-mail. This was in response to my wife's contact with him on the Internet:

> "Hi Margy! I am doing the best I can right now—I want to share something with you. First of all, I was a stubborn hardhead when I was at the Gates of Life. I loved the Lord and I wanted to do what was right by the Lord ever since I went to LTI in Louisiana. I also, at the same time, could not understand why my mother didn't want anything to do with me. I loved her with all that I was, and wanted her to hold me and tell me that she loved me the same way. I found out she had hatred for me that she could not explain to me or even discuss with me. I turned to you and Sonny for the answers and you showed me that the love the Lord has for me is more than enough to take away the pain of not having a loving mother. When I went to Detroit to live with my uncle and my grandmother, I found all the love and caring for me and my well-being that I had been looking for from my own family. This is what I missed while growing up in a reform school. I know it wasn't what the Lord wanted for me, but at the same time, I was able to share some of what I have learned from you and Sonny. I was hoping that I had done well with you guys in the Lord's eyes. I was also, at the same time, curious about life in the real world and the freedom I had never felt before. I was looking for comfort from the pain I was feeling inside and the devil was more than ready to show me things I would have never gotten myself into.

I now have seven children that I love with all my heart, and out of the seven only one will talk to me. This is my oldest son, James Aaron. Yes, I named him after your son-in-law, Aaron Ward. My children have rejected me because they said I was never there for them. They said I worked too much and they were always with the sitters."

This is a sad story, but it is the story I've heard over and over in almost 50 years of ministry. I believe that young man, if he follows the instructions I gave him over the phone, will find the help he needs in a relationship with Jesus Christ.

Spencer Cody

Probably one of the most interesting stories of all was about Spencer Cody, a young Kiowa Indian from Oklahoma. Spencer had a heavy drinking problem like a lot of the Indians. He had called all around trying to find someone to help with his problem. He had no luck until he called Gates of Life. As Spencer told me his story, I felt the Lord quicken me to take Spencer and his family into our ministry to try and help them. That was a new experience for us. We had never had to provide for a whole family. Spencer was married girl and had two little children. We provided a place for them to live in the area, and Spencer began to work for our fence company. We provided for his expenses and gave constant supervision, as much as possible. Since he lived off campus, we could not provide absolute accountability. One night, his wife Becky called and told me Spencer was in jail. He had gotten drunk and they found him parked on the side of the road with one of his children with him. She wanted me to go and see him in jail. I felt sorry for her, so I went to the jail in Quitman and got Spencer out. I knew at that point that Spencer needed a complete deliverance from his addiction to alcohol. I believe the real deliverance came for Spencer one day while working on the fence line with Ed Milewski, our foreman. Last Days Ministry published Spencer's story that follows as a tract.

A Kiowa Son

"I sat looking at the white man sitting a few feet away from me. My heart was cold towards this man and I assumed that he felt the same way about me. It seems like this was the way it had always been, and the way it would always be, with the Indian and the white man as enemies, facing each other in anger and suspicion. This man, Sonny, had taken me into his home to help me overcome my addiction to alcohol. But Sonny had opened his home to other men who needed help, and now I realized that I had placed myself in the midst of the very thing I hated most; white man. I could've left, but I didn't have any other option in my life at this point. Things had gone well at first. I kept to myself and just tried to do what was requested of me. But one day, we were all building fences and one of the other men began to antagonize me. Cold fury began to well up within me and before I knew it, I was beating him mercilessly with my fist. He had fallen to the ground, moaning in pain, and I continued to kick him again and again until blood was flowing from his face and ear. I had intended to crush the life from him, but for some reason, I had stopped. Later, when we arrived back at Sonny's house, I still couldn't understand what had stopped me from murdering the other man. Sonny called me into his office and I thought to myself, if this white man provokes me, I'm going to hurt him. He didn't say anything at first, but just

sat there looking at me, incredulous at the amount of anger and hatred that had been pouring out of me. Sonny kept shaking his head in disbelief, saying, "I just can't understand why you reacted that way!" He paused for a moment and then a look of realization spread across his face. He blurted out, "Spencer, you have hatred and bitterness in your heart towards white people!"

I looked at him and said coldly, "Yeah, you're right, and I don't think I like you that much either." I wanted him to react to my words, but he did nothing. A few seconds before, I had expected Sonny to try and intimidate me as other white men had always done. Instead, I felt strangely uneasy. "Why?" He pleaded, "Why are you so angry?"

In that moment, my mind wandered back to my childhood days in Oklahoma and to my father. My father was a Kiowa Indian who loved Jesus. As a young man, he had been an alcoholic, but was miraculously saved on a Skid Row street in Los Angeles. He came home to Oklahoma, married my mother and said to himself, "Who lives in the white man's world, I will need to be like a white man." So he went off to college and got his degree in accounting. We came back to Oklahoma, but no one would hire him because he was an Indian. He tried and tried to find work, but no one would even talk to him. So he took a job as a dishwasher. My father had a college degree, yet he worked in that kitchen washing dishes until he died. My father would always go to church at the Indian mission down the street, but most of the time he had been the only one there. Preachers for the Indians were few and far between (The Last Days, 1994)."

Spencer told me how he accepted Jesus as a teen. He went to Bible College and got an associate degree and began to preach. They went back to the high school and began to win souls on the school campus. He married a white girl and tried to fit in to the white man's culture, but he just could not quit the drinking. Spencer rebelled against God when the white church he attended split. It was then that he walked away from God and became engulfed in his drinking once again. His father died, and at the gravesite he said to his father, "I'll see you in heaven." Once again he turned back to Jesus. Spencer was so addicted to alcohol, he was drinking a fifth of whiskey a day. He ended up in a Native American detoxification center, but could only stay there for a few months. That's when he found Gates of Life. He did not realize that it was the beginning of the end of his long bitter journey to freedom. As Spencer continued telling me the stories of how his father and sister were mistreated by the white man in the very prejudiced atmosphere of Lawton, Oklahoma, I couldn't fight back the tears of sorrow and guilt I felt for how his people were treated. It was as if I had taken up his hurt. I asked Spencer to forgive my family and me for how the Indians were treated. I could only speak for my family, but the Holy Spirit had sincerely touched me. Spencer could not believe that a white man could feel that way, and it touched that bitter spot in his heart. He broke into tears and said, "I forgive you." I believe that was when God set him free from alcohol. He was a changed man. After Spencer's deliverance, he had two brothers that came and went through our ministry. Mike and Mark Cody were saved and delivered. Praise God Spencer was one of many who had been sent to us by God. Some were delivered, and some weren't. All had one thing in common; their hearts were eaten up with bitterness and resentment. To tell the story behind all the men who came to the ministry would take another whole book, so I will share just a few of their stories.

John

One was a young man named John, sixteen years old when his mother brought him to us. He was involved with drugs and other things, and she could not handle him. It was our policy not to take anyone under eighteen years of age, nevertheless, I felt really sorry for her so we agreed to take him in. Naturally, he didn't want to be with us, and we had a real battle on our hands. John told his story in our newsletter:

> "When I came to the Gates of Life, I had no intention of serving God. Having lived my own way for so long, I didn't think it was possible for me to change, and because of past hurts and problems, I harbored deep bitterness toward authority. Running wild and doing my own thing, I continually found myself in and out of juvenile detention centers on charges of drug abuse, running away from home, and various other things.
>
> Since I had never learned to deal with my problems, I used drugs as a way of escape and based my life on getting my own way by conning others.
>
> My parents and the law almost completely gave up on me and they were using Gates of Life as a last resort. My probation officer gave me the choice between Gates of Life or a correctional institution. So in February, 1982, I was probated to this ministry. At first, as you can imagine, times were hard and I was miserable. That was a real spiritual battle going on inside of me, and it was for my soul. My concept of the Lord was so demented that it didn't look as though I would make it, but because of the love of God working through the directors and the staff at Gates of Life, I started to question my way of living. God's character

was shown to me in a practical and sensible way by their kindness. Looking back at my past life, I started to see that all the problems I had were because of my wrong choices. It says in Galatians 6:7-8 in the King James Version, 'Be not deceived; God is not mocked; ... for whatsoever a man soweth to his flesh shall of the flesh reap corruption; but he that soweth to the Spirit shall of the Spirit reap life everlasting.' Reading this, I saw that my life needed to change. Since Gates of Life is built on godly principles and its atmosphere is that of a family, I have learned to deal with my problems when they come up, and not only the problems but also the attitudes that caused the problems. God really had hold of my life, and because of this, I have seen relationships between my parents and numerous other people restored to me once again. God has been good to me! I now have the desire to see others' lives changed through my example (Gates of Life, 1983)."

After I officiated at John's wedding in his marriage to a girl from Philadelphia, John moved away. He came back many years and five children later to visit me. He had become an accomplished guitar player and singer. I invited him to my Bible class to minister to them. He gave us some very inspirational music and testimony that blessed not only me, but all my class.

Gregg Jensky

Gregg Jensky has been part of our family and a close friend for over 30 years. Gregg's story appeared in our newsletter in 1982 as follows:

"In 1976, I was seeing three psychiatrists and all of them were telling me I would have to learn to live with my problem. Somehow, I knew that wasn't right. About that time, I met some Christians in Denver, Colorado, who told me what I knew was the truth: that Jesus could change both me and my problem. Right then I gave my life to Him. Soon after, I went through a Christian training school, and afterwards worked full time with a ministry for about six months. An incident happened which resulted in my leaving that ministry. I went to Oregon and was there about three years, and lived pretty much in a backslidden condition. I knew the Lord wanted me to go back and get things straightened out, but because of hard feelings, I resisted. Finally, some friends at the ministry I had left invited me to come back and visit, and the process of healing really began. I later attended a discipleship training program in Tacoma, Washington, and from there, I was led to become part of Gates of Life in Texas. Since coming home in June, 1980, I have learned, more than anything else, about love. Because Gates of Life is a family-oriented ministry, it has helped me learn how to see and love people on a one-to-one basis. I've also been learning to care for others' needs, even before my own; in other words, preferring one another in love (Gates of Life Newsletter, 1982)."

After six months with the ministry of Gates of Life, Gregg became part of the staff. He established a cleaning business and odd-jobs service that supported our ministry for years. Gregg served in a local church in the Lindale area until returning home to California to help take care of his elderly mother.

Charlie Morgan

Probably one of the most troubling stories of all was the story of Charlie Morgan. Charlie was brought to us by one of David Wilkerson's staff members. He was picked up while hitchhiking on Interstate 45. I don't remember the full details of the story he told us about his dad; I just know it was not the truth. After about four days with us, the Holy Spirit began to move on him. He confessed that he had stolen money from his employer while working in Reading, Pennsylvania. After taking the money, he went to Las Vegas and spent the money on gambling and partying. Then he started hitchhiking toward Texas.

Charlie was a very talented young man. He could play the piano and sing like Frank Sinatra. He was also good with his hands; he could build anything he put his mind to. Charlie immediately fit in our family. We grew to love him very much as a member of the church body. After approximately seven months with us, he left suddenly in the night and we had no idea where he was going. Margy and I were deeply hurt by this unexpected move. We called his mother and told her what had happened and asked her to let us know if she heard from him. It was not very long before she called us and told us that Charlie had called her from jail in Phoenix, Arizona. Margy and I caught a flight to Phoenix to see Charlie and find out why he had left.

Charlie was shocked to see that we had come all the way from Texas to visit him in jail. He told us he left to hitchhike to California where his mother was, but he was picked up by the police for the theft of his employer's money. While we had made contact with the employer in Reading, Pennsylvania, and Charlie had begun to pay back the money he had stolen, we had failed to notify the police, so there was still a warrant out for his arrest. After I explained to the police about our ministry, they released him into our custody. We flew back to Texas and made arrangements to fly Charlie and me to Reading, Pennsylvania, to face the charges they had against him. We arrived there at 8 a.m. in the morning with no attorneys and not knowing anyone there. We went to the D.A.'s office and he told us to go to the courtroom and wait until he called us. So we did just that. It must have been close to twelve o'clock before the judge called us before him. The judge looked at me and said, "Are you from Texas? If so, where is your hat?"

I told him that I left my hat at home, but I did have my cowboy boots on. The courtroom laughed. The judge then said there were a lot of people in Reading that thought they were cowboys, but they were just Berks County fools. The whole courtroom broke out in laughter. The judge then turned to Charlie and asked him if he wanted to go back to Gates of Life. Of course Charlie replied, "Yes, sir."

The judge then said, "I sentence you, Charley Morgan, to five years in the Gates of Life ministry. Charley was really happy with that sentence, and who wouldn't be since he had been facing five years in the penitentiary. Charlie wrote this poem about the ministry of Gates of Life in 1981.

Gates of Life by Charlie Morgan

"Sometimes I turn around to see reality within That not so long ago in me dwelt Satan's rotten sin. A walking dead man I became because of greed and hate. A place of pain and emptiness, would this become my fate? I knew nothing of the peaceful mind a conscience satisfied I knew though that a man had come for these things and he had died. To save me from myself no less for me I had despised, Instead of death I met someone who brought not pain but life. I

found people just like Him who loved me with their lives, who showed me more of righteousness than I had realized, who love me as their own beloved son no matter what I did. That even when I turned away, they showed me God's love instead. But I knew not what lie ahead if I followed his advice, But he brought before my thirsting eyes a place of trials at first despised. Then I came to realize, he brought me to his Gates of Life."

Ken Dustin

Ken Dustin was one of our boys, and I called them our boys because that was the way we felt. Everyone always called him "The Dust." When Ken arrived at the airport in Tyler, Texas, I went to pick him up. Ken was a new Christian, sent to us by his youth leader in Cleveland, Ohio. When Ken got off the plane, I was looking at a genuine nerd. He wore his pants high around his waist and too short, revealing his multicolored tennis shoes and socks. Although Ken was awkward and uncoordinated, we found he could play the piano quite well and could also carry a tune. It wasn't long before he became part of our traveling singing group. When we were not traveling, he worked with Ed and Aaron on the work crew. After being here a while, he hooked up with John Davis and together they decided to run away. They slipped out one night and hitchhiked to Greenville, Texas, not far away. Greenville was where John was from. They got picked up and put in jail in Greenville. Margy got a phone call from Ken one night asking if we could come pick him up. Using tough love, Margy told him to get back to Gates the same way he got to Greenville. So Ken hitchhiked back to Mineola, a small town just north of where the ministry is, and Margy picked him up there. The experience opened Ken's eyes. He went on to become one of our success stories. After spending time here at Gates, he enrolled in a local college and moved into town. Ken later got a job in the computer field and met a young lady who became his wife.

Not too long ago, Ken came to visit us in his own private plane. He flew all the way from Boston and landed in Mineola's small airport. It was wonderful to see that young man grown up and successful. He spent the night with us and attended church with us. I can't explain the joy Margy and I had to see him, and that he cared enough to visit with us. He later emailed these encouraging words: *"Thank you, Sonny and Margy, for a great time. Gates of Life was the best thing that ever happened to me."* Margy and I wished that all of our stories were like that one, but unfortunately, they were not.

Danny Dawson

Another one of the guys who came to our program was Danny Dawson, a local boy from Mineola. Danny graduated from Mineola High School and was, for the most part, a good kid. After graduating from high school, Danny experimented with drugs and got hooked. Danny had a good job working at the railroad with his dad. When his habit became bad enough that they told him to get help, his parents brought him to our ministry. Danny did real well while working here. He was very cooperative and worked well in the fence company. He went through the ministry and was released back to his railroad job. He bought a new truck and seemed to be doing well, but he ran into some old friends and took one hit of crack cocaine and was back on the habit. Once again Danny showed up at the ministry in really bad shape. He was skin and bones, and his health was failing. We took him back into the program, and once more Danny did well. His health soon returned to him. After leaving the ministry in good health, he got a good job and was doing very well, but he got back on drugs again. At that time, Margy and I had moved to Florida to be a part of Steve Hill's ministry and the revival that was going on in Pensacola. Danny's mom called us and asked if there was anything we could do. Danny's liver was shutting down and he was at the brink of death because of his addiction to drugs. We told her to bring him to Florida to the revival for prayer. After getting there, they brought Danny to the service. I got Steve Hill and Pastor Kilpatrick to pray for him. Danny said that after they prayed for him, the taste and the smell of drugs left him. Danny quit doing drugs. He has a good trucking business going and has a wife and a nice home. He is a member of the Church on the Rock in Quitman, Texas, where he met his wife.

Ann Roberts

Another person that we housed was Ann Roberts. She became like a daughter to us, and visits frequently. We first met Ann in youth camp in 1967. I don't remember much about her at that time, just that she was part of that camp. In 1976, we were running a ministry in Houston for Agape Force. At the coffeehouse there, we came in contact with Ann again. She was a very outgoing and likable person, so we clicked right away. Ann was going through a lot of hurt and disappointment because of a relationship, and she was battling alcohol addiction. She also had an alcoholic father. We convinced her to go through a discipleship program at the Agape Force ranch in Lindale, Texas.

Ann went through the training and was placed in one of the Agape Force ministries. She later left the ministry and went to Florida. We stayed in contact with her, but could tell she was not happy and had returned to drinking once again. We often talked to her about moving back to Texas before she finally gave in. She moved in with us, became part of our family, and worked well in the office at our fence company. She later received complete deliverance through a ministry in Mexico with our longtime friend, Robert Duran. Ann has been living in victory to this day. She got a good job working in Frisco, outside of Dallas. She became part of a local church there—daily blessed by God. All the folks at that church seem to love her a lot.

Salvador Ramos

Another one of our guys was Salvador Ramos, originally from Guatemala. Some Agape Force friends near Kerrville, Texas, referred him to us. My friends met him when they went to visit him in jail, where he was incarcerated. After his release, he moved in with us. He seemed to fit in well and later became a faithful friend and good employee of Gateway Fence Company. Salvador was blessed with his own fence company and has done quite well. As far as I know, he is still attending Community Christian Fellowship.

Howard Warren

Howard Warren, a young man who graduated with our son, Brian, was another one of our guys. Howard was basically a good young man. He just wanted to be discipled. He moved in with us and worked in the business for a period of time. Howard also had a good voice so he sang with Spencer Cody, as well as David Rooker, who was a part of our singing group at one time.

Jonathan James

One of our disciples was a young man named Jonathan James, whose pastor brought him to us for discipleship. He was not on drugs, but did need help. I'm not too sure how long Jonathan lived with us, but I know it was more than a year. After leaving the program, he worked with the fence company as an employee for a while. At one point, he was overseeing the work at the concrete plant, where we produced the concrete material. After we dissolved the business and ministry and moved to Pensacola, he got engaged and married the daughter of the new pastor at Community Christian Fellowship. He became a member of that church and they have had children.

Burt Forney

Another one of our guys, who was a part of our ministry for quite some time, was Burt Forney. Burt was a very intelligent young man who had his own successful cleaning business. Our local dentist brought him to us because he was facing jail time for writing his own prescriptions for drugs. He had a serious addiction. Burt immediately fit into our program and became quite an asset to the ministry. He also was part of our singing group and traveled with us for a while. Burt later became interested in one of the young ladies who was in the Agape Force group called Silver Wind. They got engaged and I soon found myself traveling to Tacoma, Washington, to perform their marriage. Burt is now one of the elders at Community Christian Fellowship. With David Hickey as pastor, that church has grown over the years to around 1,000 in attendance on Sunday.

Todd Pruett

Todd Pruett is another young man that stands out in my mind who came to us to be discipled. Todd was a very hard worker and contributed not only a good example of a servant's heart, but also an excellent working attitude. You can tell a lot about a person's character by the way he works. Todd spent some time with us, and then married one of the girls that he met at Community Christian Fellowship (CCF). I performed the ceremony in the cold state of Wisconsin. Later, he attended the Brownsville School of Ministry and served as a missionary to Thailand for ten years. He is currently back at CCF, but still traveling to Thailand occasionally for Fire Ministries. He has four children—three of which are teenagers.

Stanley Mote

Another one of the men who was with our ministry was a young man named Stanley Mote. Stanley was an Indian from a small town in Kansas. One of the guys picked him up, while he was hitchhiking on the highway. Like always we were open to take him in. Stanley was from a very dysfunctional family. As far as we could tell, he had no contact with his biological family. He told us about how as a small children, he and his brother, who we never met, would survive by eating out of the dumpster next to a fast food restaurant. As he would tell stories about their survival, he wept with tears of anguish streaming down his face. We did all we could to show the love of Jesus to Stanley. We bought him clothes, since he didn't have any except what was on his back. Sometimes he left in the night, not taking anything with him. I believe he was tormented in his sleep. Later he would show back up with nothing except the clothes on his back. One time, he called us from a small town in Kansas and told us he was going to kill himself. I took one of the guys and we drove all the way to Kansas to see if we could stop him. We visited him for a few days and when we left, he seemed all right. A couple of weeks later, I received a phone call from him during the night. He said he was in Dallas and that he was coming to kill me. I waited up all night for him, but he never showed up. I have never heard from him since. I often wonder whatever happened to that hurting young man, hoping that the witness he received while here would someday set him free.

Dutch

Dutch was another of the guys that were picked up on the highway. He was a young man who acted like an old man. He had a long scraggly beard and hair, and he walked very slowly. He had experience building chain-link fence, so we put him to work with the fence crew. After Dutch was with us for a while, we were able to get him to shave his beard and cut his hair. What a remarkable change that made in his appearance. He was a very handsome young man. I took him to Seabrook to visit an old employer, and to visit his mother. When we arrived at the employer's door he could not believe the changes in Dutch's appearance. Unfortunately the change did not last long; Dutch soon left and went back to hitchhiking on the road. He returned from time to time, but still had that restless attitude.

Paul

There is one other person I would like to mention, but I will change the name to protect the innocent. I will call him Paul. We met Paul while witnessing on the streets in downtown Tyler.

One of our men talked to him and prayed with him on the sidewalk. It seemed that he was having problems in his marriage. I don't remember the details, but we tried to help him. I think at that time he also had a problem with alcohol. We located a place near us where he and his wife could move in and we could minister to them. That did not last long; he ended up moving away. The next thing I knew, he appeared at our door at 2 a.m. one morning. Everyone was asleep, so Greg let him in and then woke me up. He went back to sleep and left me with that guy in the living room. I asked, "Paul, what can I do for you?" He said, "I came here to kill you." He had a loaded pistol in his pocket. I said, "Paul, why do you want to kill me?" He had no reason. I told him that all we wanted to do was help him. I think that he had been drinking quite a lot, so I continued to reason with him. All the time I was thinking about how I could grab the gun from that big broad-shouldered hulk. I finally talked him out of it and then offered him a ride home, but he said he had left his car down the road. The next time we heard anything about Paul, he had held someone captive in downtown Tyler. We later heard that he went to prison.

A Rebellious 18-year-old

One incident that stands out happened when we took in an eighteen-year-old who was totally rebellious. He acted like a spoiled kid, and many times was almost impossible to work with. After dealing with his rebellious attitude for some time, I was about ready to give up on him. Since we could not lay a hand on him, it was difficult to figure out a way to discipline him.

One day I came up with an idea of how I might reach him. I've forgotten what he had done, but I was at my wits end when I marched him to the back of the property. I begin to strip a long switch out of a limb from a bush. He watched me, obviously wondering what I was going to do with that large switch. I handed it to him, and bent over telling him to give me five strong licks with that switch. He said, "I can't do that."

I told him that he better hit me and hit me hard or I would use it on him. Then he began to strike me, at first lightly, and then harder and harder. I was almost sorry that I had thought of that as a discipline, but when he finished, he was bawling like a baby. I told him that was what Jesus did for us on the cross. He took the punishment that we rightly deserved so we could be reunited with our Lord. I believe for the first time he got the point, and I was happy.

CHAPTER 13
Our Children

SOME OF THE most fun-filled times we had at the Gates of Life were at Thanksgiving and Christmas. Our whole family gathered at the ministry house, along with the men and other guests, for a wonderful time of fellowship and food. Some of our guests included Winkey Pratney and his wife Faeona, and others that had no family to go to. We thoroughly enjoyed these opportunities to share our family with others As our three oldest granddaughters grew, they would dress up in their grandma's old clothes and put on a show for us. They were very entertaining and everyone seemed to enjoy seeing them show off.

Our children's names and birth dates, in order, are:

Our firstborn, Claude Michael Jaynes, was born in the US Naval Hospital at Camp Pendleton, California, on June 9, 1956. Although his first name was Claude, we called him Mike. He was a cute little thing and was walking by the time he was one year old. Mike grew up fast. It seemed the time flew by and he was soon enrolled at Spring Junior High in Spring, Texas.

I'll never forget the time he came home and said he had joined the football team. Mike was not a very big person, so I found it hard to believe he could make the team. He was a defensive back and did quite well in that position. I don't think I ever missed a game. One game that stands out in my memory was when they played an all-black school in Crosby, Texas. It poured down rain during the whole game and we stayed to the bitter end. Our team lost and the score was 75 to 0. I also remember a game where Mike intercepted a pass and ran twenty-five yards for a touchdown. I jumped up and down with excitement. When they mispronounced his name, I quickly went to the press box and let them know what his name was. Mike also excelled in drama. He played the lead role in the musical, Bye-bye Birdie. He played Conrad Birdie and rode a motorcycle down the center of the auditorium and onto the stage. Mike was the president of the ninth, tenth, and eleventh grades, and was elected vice president of the student body during his senior year. He was a good student in school despite one of his teachers saying he would never do well because of his dyslexia. He was also a lifeguard in our youth camps where our whole family volunteered. At one of our camps, he was voted best camper. Mike was a good kid; I never had any major problems with him.

After he became part of the Agape Force with the rest of the family, he led an Agape Force production called Ginger Brook Fare. That was a team of clowns that traveled to churches and other events, teaching children character qualities through a series of musicals. Mike was the head clown and was a teacher in Mik's Clown Training School. The clowns could earn their red noses by learning character qualities such as truthfulness. That production became quite successful and they soon made three videos for Word Records. After leaving the ministry, Mike put together a tour of the award-winning production, Music

Machine. He traveled several states with over twenty-eight people in the cast. It was quite a production. Mike displayed multiple talents as he became quite good in the area of makeup as well. One time when he was going to church in Dallas, the pastor requested that he make himself up to look like a homeless bum to fit into his pastor's sermon that day. Margy and I attended the service to witness our son, Brian's, baptism. When we arrived, we noticed that Mike was nowhere around. I began to get a little angry that Mike was not there to see his brother baptized. As the service began, and just before Brian was to be baptized, an old, rugged looking bum came into the church and sat down not too far from where we were. He began to make noise, moving around in his chair, disturbing the whole service. I began to get angry and I leaned over and told my wife, "Somebody needs to get that bum out of here."

Pretty soon the bum moved up to the front row, continuing to squirm and make noise. Finally, some elders led the bum out the door. I didn't know until later that it was Mike, illustrating the sermon concerning how we treat the unlovely that come into our church. Of course, I failed the test miserably and I had to repent.

Mike played the same role years later while attending New Life Worship Center where I was on staff. Our church responded very well. They saw him wandering around outside and they invited him in. They offered him chief seats and they collected money to help him out. Several people invited him to dinner. I was very proud to hear about that. I hadn't been aware that the pastor had asked him to play that role that time either.

Mike met a girl in the Agape Force and they were soon married in Minneapolis, Minnesota. Her name was Judy Welch. I performed the wedding and it was my first duty after receiving my first ordination, which was from Agape Force. Times were hard on Mike during that phase of life, trying to fulfill his commitment to the ministry and supporting his family. By that time, he had left the Agape Force and was traveling with Music Machine. He had two children: Christina born March 10, 1982, and Tiffany born June 16, 1983. I was present at both of these births. Mike eventually left the ministry to pursue a career in the automobile business. He became quite successful at that business, which would become his main source of income for years to come. Although Mike had to leave the ministry to support his family, he never left the idea of being in the ministry.

On February 7, 1987, along came Mike's third child, Nicholas. Following Nicholas was Emily, who was born March 15, 1988. After Emily came the arrival of Mike's fifth child Andrew, born April 9, 1991. That would end Mike's family expansion. There were some events that followed that were hurtful to all of us, but I won't go into details. Mike and Judy eventually divorced, and Mike remarried and continued to work in a local Ford dealership. He also helped his younger brother in the movie business, doing art direction and special effects. Mike also ran for the city council in Winnsboro, Texas.

Our second child, Cynthia Jean, was born Sept. 16, 1957. She was a cutie. Some of my favorite pictures of her while she was a baby were of her playing in the mud. Like Mike, she went to Spring High School in Spring, Texas, where the family lived for eight years before going to California. Cindy was active in sports, including track and basketball. She was active in youth camps and was a lifeguard, along with Mike. Cindy graduated from a school in California. She traveled with the girls' singing group while in the Agape Force. Cindy, a talented musician, took seven years of progressive piano and could sing quite well. She later married Aaron Ward, one of the wonderful guys at Gates of Life. They both settled down into helping in our ministry at the Gates of Life and Gateway Fence Company.

Cindy has three children: Ashlee was born August 24, 1982; Josh was born March 31, 1987; and Whitney was born April 2, 1990. She is still happily married to Aaron, who now works for a local contractor and builds boats on the side.

After her children were grown, Cindy went on to finish nursing school and became a nurse at Trinity Mother Frances Hospital in Tyler. She has begun pursuing her master's degree in order to teach nursing.

Our third child, Brian Thomas Jaynes, was born November 24, 1964. Brian started school when he was four at a private Christian school in Conroe, Texas, where his mom, Margy, worked. He was always a good student. After we moved to California, Brian attended the local school in Sebastopol. Later, we moved back to Texas where, in the seventh grade, Brian started playing football. He was very active in all sports such as football, track, and basketball, but football was his main sport. Of course, I never missed a game. While he was in the seventh and eighth grade, I still worked at the docks in Houston off and on, so sometimes I had to drive from Houston to Lindale to attend the football games. The greatest entertainment in my life was watching my kids play sports. Brian also had acting and singing talents. He played the part of a judge in a popular play called Inherit the Wind.

After finishing high school, Brian went to junior college in Tyler. While working at Dillard's clothing department, he met a guy who had an influential job in the oilfield business. He talked Brian into going to work for them in Longview, Texas. After a while, Brian wanted to move into an apartment there in Longview. That was a sad time for my wife and me. We would soon be empty nesters. We began to get some necessary things together for cooking his meals and we helped him move.

Although we had an active ministry going, we knew we would miss our son. There is still hurt even now, but after many tears and prayers, we released him to a new life with our blessings. Brian ended up calling us after several months and wanted to come back home. We moved him back and he soon went on the road with his brother, Mike, working with the traveling production of the award-winning children's album, The Music Machine.

Later, Brian moved to Dallas to seek his direction in life. He followed his brother in the automobile business and they both became quite successful. Later, Brian moved to California to pursue another direction for his life. He is now back in Lindale, Texas, with his wife, Jennifer. She has given him two of the cutest twins you will ever see: Brian Christopher and Ryan Ezekiel. They have been a great joy to the whole family, but especially to their grandmother and grandpa. Brian Christopher was born with a heart problem and by the time he was 3 ½ years old, he'd had three open-heart surgeries. With much loving care by their mother and father, and the prayers of everyone at home and at church, little Christopher is well and happy. Their mother, Jennifer, has been a wonderful, caring mother. She has made sure that the boys have the best and healthiest food she could make. She has even written her own children's recipe book.

Margy and I consider ourselves greatly blessed to have all our children and grandchildren right in the Tyler area. God has blessed us with a wonderful family. We pray regularly for all our children, grandchildren, and great-grandchildren. Our prayer is that they will find peace and joy, as we have, in Jesus Christ. Our commitment to Jesus and our local church has kept us through many trials.

Our great-grandchildren are Triston Hicks, Jori'l Hicks, Mekayla Hicks, Tres Taylor, Zane Taylor, Henry Edison Persing, Brighton Noelle Persing, and Lucy Benét Jaynes.

Some of the greatest times we have had are getting together with all the children and grandchildren on special occasions at the Gates of Life house in Garden Valley, Texas. At one point, Margy and I were headed to Kansas City for a conference at the Kansas City church. We did not have a decent car for the trip, so we decided to go through Fort Worth where Michael and Brian worked at a local new-car dealership. Brian was a sales manager at the Mitsubishi dealership, so we stopped by to see if he could lend us a car for the trip. We also wanted him to find us a good used car that we could trade our old junker in for. I told Brian I only had $2,000, and that's all I wanted to pay in order to stay out of debt. He let us drive one of their demos for the trip and said that he would look for a car for us. Our trip to Kansas City was a blessing we enjoyed and found spiritually invigorating. After the conference, we got back to Fort Worth to deliver the car and see if he had found us a good used car. Mike was visiting his brother at the dealership when we arrived, and he and Brian wanted me to drive a brand new Mitsubishi Gallant. I kept telling them I did not want to go into debt for a car, but they insisted I drive this new car. So I did, and when Margy and I got back they asked how I liked the car. Of course it was nice to drive a new car, but I kept insisting that I was not going into debt. They then told me the two of them, together, wanted to buy the car for me. At first I said, "No way." But I heard that still small voice that had consistently spoken to me in my spirit say, "Let them wash your feet." So I gave in and consented to allow them to sign me up for that new car. That was another blessing from God in our lives.

When Margy and I returned home, we had a message on our phone that my mom was in the hospital in Houston, not expected to live through the night. I got a flight out of Tyler to Houston immediately, and went to see my mom. I went to her bedside and she was in ICU, lying there all swollen with tubes sticking out all over. I grabbed her hand and asked her if she had made things right with God. My mom had lived in a backslidden state for several years. She had become successful in selling Stanley Home Products and had turned her back on God. She had taken up drinking and gambling. She told me herself that she was hooked on whiskey and sometimes drank a fifth of whiskey at night to go to sleep. When I asked her if she had made things right with God, she smiled and nodded her head as if to say, "Yes." I prayed a short prayer. "God, if you are finished with my mom, take her life. We release her into your hands. But if you have more for her to do, spare her life." I then left the room and went to wait in the waiting room with the rest of the family. We were there for a short while when the doctor came in looking very serious. He said, "Your mom has sealed her fate. She has removed all the life support herself and I do not think it will be long before she dies." What he did not know was that God had other plans. By midmorning the next day, they had taken her out of ICU and placed her in a regular room. She preached to everyone that came into that room. Her message was, "If God can save a wicked old lady like me, He can save you. You better get saved!"

My mom lived for 10 more years, the precious picture of a changed woman. She began to call all her friends she used to drink and gamble with. She told them what God had done for her, He could do for them. She died in 1999. My father died in his sleep several years before she did.

While Brian was working at the dealership in Fort Worth, he called me one day very excited and asked me to read Hebrews chapter 13. Then he told me this interesting story. Brian and some of his fellow workers stood outside the dealership, being bored because it was a slow day, and telling racial jokes when an old beat-up pickup truck pulled into the lot. An old rugged-looking black man drove the truck. He got out and walked up to my Brian and asked him if he could clean toilets or sweep the floors to earn money for gas. He told my son that he was a *"minister of holiness"* and he was headed somewhere for a speaking engagement. Brian told him he would give him some gas, and for him to pull over to the gas pump. As he was attempting to fill his tank he noticed that it was not taking any gas. He turned to the man and told him, "Your tank is full!" The old man replied with a smile, "Imagine that."

My son thought that was very strange. He then asked the old man if he was hungry. The guy said, "Yes, as a matter fact I am." My son reached into his pocket and pulled out the only five-dollar bill he had, and handed it to the man. As the man took the money, he took hold of my son's hand and looked into his eyes. My son noticed that he had deep blue eyes. The man then said, "Can I pray for you?" Then he prayed this simple prayer, "Father, this is a good man. Would you bless him and bless this company."

The man got into his truck while Brian stood there in wonder. Then my son walked over to the truck and asked the man his name. "Does that really matter?" the man said. "Do you have a Bible?" My son replied, "I could get one."

The man told him to look up Hebrews chapter 13 and begin reading, and he drove off. Brian went to a phone and called me. He said, "Dad, you have a Bible."

I said, "Yes."

He said, "Look up Hebrews 13 and begin reading. I already knew Hebrews 13:2, so I paraphrased, "Be careful when you entertain strangers lest you entertain angels unaware."

Brian knew that he had heard from an angel. Up to that time, the dealership had no business for that day, but by the end of the day, they had sold more cars then they recently had before. One guy came in and said that something told him to come there to buy a car. He ended up buying two cars that day. I think he was a dentist. The next day Brian was listening to a talk show on the radio, and they were talking about angels. Brian called in and told them about his experience. The talk show host did not believe him, but Brian said, "I don't care what you believe; I know what happened." That was an experience we would remember for years to come. I don't know if Brian ever read the rest of that chapter, for if he had, it would contain some serious instruction.

I received a present from Brian for Father's Day in 1992. It was a plaque that hangs on my wall in my office. It started like this:

> *"My Father, as far back as I can remember, you've been there for me. You unselfishly provided a home, family, and love. You took special care to ensure our comfort at little thought for your own. I will always be grateful to you, my father, my friend. I always knew I could count on you to show up at every game. One look into the crowd and I would see your face, rain or shine. I remember the smiles we brought to each other's faces throughout the past. I remember your love, my father, my friend. Whenever I made mistakes you always understood. You have taught me more about patience and forgiveness than I could have ever learned in a thousand lifetimes without you. You have taught me more than you will ever know. You have taught me of the love of God, my father, my friend. I know there have been many hurts and disappointments along the way and perhaps more to come. I know that we sometimes see things differently and find it hard to agree. But even through the difficult times, you have proven to be a true friend. I will love you always,*

my father, and my friend. Above all, you have taught me about life. You have taught me that there is even more to love than just sharing it with family and friends. More to loving than just those who are easy to love. You have taught me that true love reaches outside the comfortable boundaries of the home and family. For all these things, I am forever grateful to God and to you, Dad. My father and my friend. Signed—Brian June 21, 1992."

CHAPTER 14
New Ministries

BY 1996, OUR ministry seemed to be coming to an end. I can hardly find words to describe it; I just seemed to lose my enthusiasm, probably because I was getting older. I was also missing my old friend, Brother Ravenhill. I had grown close to him over approximately a ten-year relationship. Brother Leonard was a great evangelist in England, probably in the 1940s. He moved to America, I believe in 1950. He worked with several ministries like Teen Challenge and Bethany Fellowship in Minnesota. He wrote many popular books, one in particular was entitled, Why Revival Tarries. He also wrote several other books like, Revival Praying, Revival God's Way, and America is Too Young to Die. I believe that my association with Brother Leonard triggered a hunger for revival in my life, and in the church. Revival was a central theme of all Len's prayers. If you have ever read his books, you have seen what I'm talking about. Those in our ministry, Gates of Life, became close friends with Brother Len. He was like a father and a mentor to me. I really became excited when I heard that Leonard personally knew A. W. Tozer. Dr. Tozer had written several books, all of which I had read. His writings made a deep impression on my life. I believe if a book does not inspire you to change, then it is not worth reading. Brother Leonard died in 1994, but the passion for revival continued to burn in my heart. Just a few years prior to Len's death, I met Steve Hill, a young missionary evangelist. Steve had moved to Van, Texas, and set up his office. He visited our church and I immediately connected with him because of his passion for souls.

One night, just before Leonard died, I had a dream. Most of the time, I do not have dreams that I can identify the next morning, but this dream was different. In this dream, I escorted Brother Leonard to a meeting as I had often done. The meeting was in a shopping mall, but it was a different kind of mall. When we got there, we went to a large auditorium that looked like a theater. There was no one there, so I left Len seated in a seat near the front while I went to the restroom. I had to walk the length of the mall, and as I walked I noticed on both sides of the mall there were different ministries. It was a shopping mall of churches. One could pick out whatever church fit their fancy. Kind of like it is today. When I returned to Leonard, he was gone. He was nowhere to be found. I could hear sirens sounding an alarm throughout the building. The announcer on a loudspeaker warned everyone that storms were in the area. He told us that if we followed instructions, we would be able to weather the storms. I found a place where it seemed safe and fell flat on my face. I covered my head and peeked around to see what was happening. I saw little tornadoes touching down all around me, but none came near me. When I woke from the dream, the lyrics to an old song came to my mind, "Keep me safe till the storm passes by." I asked the Lord what the dream meant and I believe He told me, "Sonny, you will be going through a series of storms. If you will follow my instructions, you will get through the storms." I did go through a series of storms, some of them with the men that were close to me. Some of the storms were with my own children. Through all of these, I learned in a very small way what God must feel when we disappoint Him—and I learned to trust in Jesus. I also believe the impression I got was that Leonard would soon go on to be with the Lord.

In June of 1995, the evangelist, Steve Hill, returned from a trip to England where he experienced a transforming touch from God through an Anglican preacher that was experiencing a revival. He then went to Pensacola, Florida, to a Sunday meeting with Pastor Kilpatrick at the Brownsville Assembly of God Church. Pastor Kilpatrick had been a supporter of Steve's ministry for quite some time. At that Sunday service, revival broke out in his church. Because the anointing was so great, they continued the service that night. The meeting went on for weeks. Steve called Community Christian Fellowship, where I was an elder, and told us he was in revival, but I, doubting Thomas, did not trust that it was authentic. After it went on for six weeks, I decided to take one of the guys and go check it out. Jonathan James was one of the men in our ministry that went with me, and we drove to Pensacola, Florida, for a weekend. Steve preached a powerful sermon and gave an altar call. The altar quickly filled up. I had never seen people run to the altar so fast. I knew God was doing something. Tears of remorse and joy flowed down the cheeks of those running to the altar. After a prayer of commitment to Jesus, Steve invited people to come for special prayer for the anointing. The aisles quickly filled with people hungry for a touch from God. Since I was hungry for a touch from God, I went forward with everyone else. When Steve saw me, he told me to help him pray for people. As I began to pray for people,

I experienced an anointing that I had never felt before. People fell out under the power of God. The place looked like a war zone. When the people begin to exit the church, there would be people lying in the bushes outside the building. Some were too "drunk in the Spirit" to drive their cars. I had never seen anything like this in my life. It was truly a spiritual awakening. The central theme of all of Steve's preaching was repentance. That was as close to what happened on the day of Pentecost in the book of Acts that I had ever seen. In the second chapter of Acts, Peter said, "For these are not drunk, as you suppose… But this is what was spoken by the prophet Joel…" (Acts 2:15-16). I continued through 1996 to visit that amazing event as often as possible. Several times we took all the guys to visit the revival. Steve Hill made arrangements for housing for all of us, and that was a real blessing. Each visit drew me closer to the powerful outpouring of the Spirit. I continued to see people healed, marriages restored, and ministries turned around and set on fire by the power of God. I don't care what the critics say; a man with an experience is never at the mercy of a man with an argument.

During our times of visiting the revival, we stayed connected to Community Christian Fellowship. I was close friends with Pastor Tracy Hanson and still sent my tithes to the church. There seemed to be an effort to push Pastor Tracy out of the church. That concerned me greatly, so I called Tracy and asked him what was happening. By that time, he had already decided to leave the church in pursuit of a different direction. I went home for a period of time to help the other elders decide on a new pastor. After interviewing several people, we decided on David Hickey, a local guy we had been in contact with off and on for years. He still remains the pastor to this day.

In 1997 the revival was going so strong that they decided to start a Bible school to train ministers that were influenced by the revival. They named the school Brownsville Revival School of Ministry (B.R.S.M.). They started with 160 students, but the school quickly grew to over 1,200 students. After we moved to Pensacola, Steve had set Margy and me up in an apartment and was paying all of our bills. One day Steve called us and asked if we would be interested in being a part of the staff at the school. At the time, we were still connected with the Gates of Life and Gateway Fence Company. Steve made an appointment for us with Dr. Brown, the president of the school. Dr. Brown was a well-versed theologian who also spoke fluent Hebrew. I had met him years before at Leonard Ravenhill's home. Dr. Brown asked my wife and me if we would be interested in becoming part of the pastoral staff at the school of ministry. I was really excited and honored that God would open the door for me. It had to be a God thing. We still had one problem that we needed to take care of. We needed to sell the fence company, so that we could pay off all our debts. Margy and I went back to Lindale to try and sell the fence company. After several attempts to sell, we were beginning to get concerned. I did not want to leave without paying my bills. One night I woke up with cold fear gripping me. I knew at once that it was a demonic attack. I went into my office and I began to pray this phrase from the Bible, "God, you have not given us a spirit of fear, but of power, love, and a sound mind." I repeated this over and over and I got louder and louder as I prayed, and then all of a sudden the fear lifted. I went back to bed and slept very well the rest of the night. The next morning I woke up and received a phone call from Barbin Fence Company saying they were interested in purchasing our company. We had been their main competitors. After meeting with Mr. Barbin, we agreed on a settlement. I received enough money to pay all my debts, including the ministry house. It was a great blessing to be able to go back and work in the ministry at Pensacola without any debts. Margy and I then returned to Brownsville School of Ministry, where we stayed for the next seven years. That would be a blessing beyond my ability to explain. Besides ministering at the altars every night five nights a week, we also went on many outreaches, some local and some overseas. All of our trips were full of spiritual adventure. My first outreach after settling in at the school of ministry was to New Orleans, during Al Gore's campaign for the presidency. The city was packed out with people there to support him. Those were very exciting times of witnessing and preaching on the streets in New Orleans. We borrowed a big truck from a local church, which was equipped for outreach purposes. The sides of the truck would fall down and make a platform. It had a PA system built in with mics and mic stands. It was ideal for ministering in the projects—government-subsidized low- rent apartments. We put the chairs out, and began playing music loud enough for the people to hear. When the people came out of their apartments, we sang and preached to them. We met up with another Christian group that was based in New Orleans and run by a very courageous lady. When she showed up to help, she had a water gun that looked like a machine gun; it was full of anointing oil. She would go around to the apartments and squirt anointing oil on all the buildings.

We had another outreach east of New Orleans. A small church located on the bayou near the bay sponsored us. Most of the houses on that bayou were just shacks. The people that lived there were fishermen and crab trappers. We had meetings in the small church and many came to hear us. I had a friend whose name was Michael. He was a former dope addict who had been in trouble with the law. He had gotten saved and was attending the Brownsville Revival School of Ministry. He became an anointed preacher, so he would preach in the evening service. One of our meetings in New Orleans was in the French Quarter. I would set up a table next to the tarot card readers and put a sign in front of the table that read Free Psalm Reading. I laid my big Bible on the table, with a candle burning beside it. One guy came up and offered to pay me to read a Psalm. I told him it was for free, so I read the first Psalm to him. When I finished he asked me to read another, so I read the second Psalm. On our outreaches to Algiers, we usually stayed at the Youth With A Mission (YWAM) base, just across the river from the French waters. We would catch the ferry to get across the river. Sometimes we found opportunities to witness on the ferry. On one occasion, we ministered to a young man who acknowledged that he needed God. We prayed for him, and he fell out under the power of God right there on the ferryboat. We never experienced any fear. *"For God had not given us a spirit of fear, but of power and of love and of a sound mind"* (2 Timothy 1:7).

While in the school, we made several trips to Mexico that proved to be spiritually rewarding. On one trip, we went to Juarez, Mexico, and ministered in a church with maybe a couple of thousand members whose pastor was an American. They had a discipleship school run by my old friend, Robert Duran. He had about 30 students. I taught in that school on the subject of relationships. After classes, we prayed for the students and felt a strong anointing while there. Another one of our outreaches was a mission trip to the Philippines. I took about eight students from the school to Cebu. We flew from Florida to Seattle, Washington, and then on to Tokyo, where we had an eight-hour layover. From Tokyo, we flew to the Philippines. The trip, although long, was not too bad. From a doctor who taught in our school, I learned what to do on long trips overseas. When the plane took off, I would take two Tylenol PMs. That allowed me to sleep through the whole trip. After arriving in

Cebu, we were met by a team from the Cebu Teen Challenge, run by a guy named Jacob. He was an ex-drug addict who had been converted and trained through the Teen Challenge Ministry. They had a large compound just outside the main city, located high on a hill that overlooked the city. That ministry primarily reached out to the children on the streets of Cebu. It was very heartbreaking to see six- and seven-year-old children running in the streets. At night they rolled out their cardboard beds to sleep on. Jacob had a team go down to the streets to feed the children several times a week. They seemed to know when he would be there, and they would wait. What a powerful ministry! That ministry touched my heart more than any other in which I had ever been involved. I had never seen so many children sleeping on the streets with no home to go to. Jacob's team loaded up their van a couple of times a week and picked up the children. We joined his team when they brought the children to their compound, bathed them, and gave them clean clothes to wear. After cleaning them up, we took the children individually and picked the lice out of their hair. The children would then take a nap in the main building. Because the children were starved for love and affection, the ladies on my team would take a nap with them.

We also ministered in a Bible school and a small church while we were there. What a joy to see these poor people happy in the Lord, and dancing and singing with joy. The services were powerful and full of anointing. The church was held in a tent and the only bathroom was an outhouse. From the Philippines, we flew to Hawaii, and then to the island of Kauai where we ministered in the small Aloha Church Assembly of God in Lihue. The son of the pastor was a student in the school in Florida where I was on staff. This church was in the process of building a new sanctuary. Their services were being held temporarily in a tent and our team helped them finish their building. We had a great time not only ministering, but touring the island and snorkeling, and were blessed to stay in a stately home that must have been over 100 years old.

Our next trip was to Milan, Italy. One of our graduates from B.R.S.M., Alfredo, along with his wife, Sylvia, lived in Milan. He had been pastoring a small church in the city. They had a daughter named Veronica. We became good friends while he was at the school. They were great hosts as our whole team of six stayed in their apartment during the outreach. We had a wonderful time ministering in the church and on the streets. We went to the high schools and passed out tracts, and tried to speak to the students about Jesus. Alfredo and his family became even closer friends later when they moved to Tyler, Texas. They received their green cards, and Alfredo became employed at the Henderson State Prison as a chaplain. God has blessed them tremendously. We began our transition home when, after seven years at the Brownsville School of Ministry, the Lord said it was time to move back to Tyler. On our way back, we prayed that God would open up a new job in a local church where I could supplement my income. At that time, we owned a small cabin on a lake near the old Gates of Life house that the ministry owned. My son, Mike, and his family had occupied the ministry house while we were in Pensacola.

Margy and I had purchased the lot on the lake and we planned to build a home there. We had bought plans, but after getting a bid for a house, we realized it was more than we could afford and we decided not to build. We had not been living in the cabin very long when we decided to move back into the old Gates of Life house. There just was not enough room in that small cabin. We only had one closet and that was not enough for my wife, much less for the two of us. We had sold some property that the ministry owned next to the house. The sale provided a little money to fix the house up, buy new furniture, and do some remodeling. We painted the outside and the inside of the house, and by the time we got ready to move in, it looked like a new house.

We were not home very long until we got a job in Tyler at New Life, a newly formed church. Jim and Dee Patton, friends from the Agape Force days, worked there as children's pastors. They introduced us to Pastor Rudy Bond, who later decided to hire us. God answered our prayers and we served there seven years. We were pastors for the senior-adults-over-55 group. It challenged me, because I had never worked with the older generation. When I told the pastor that, he said, "Have you looked in the mirror lately?"

That was good for a laugh. I had a small committee to help plan activities for the group. We would plan trips to the rodeo, southern gospel concerts, and potluck dinners. I was also their Sunday school teacher. The job was just what I prayed for. I only had to be there three days a week. The salary was small, but enough for me to manage with Social Security and my pension from the docks. We were at New Life a short time when, as I drove to work one morning, I listened to my friend Tom Dooley's radio program, "The Journey." Tom had a popular radio voice. His syndicated Christian radio program played in more than 25 states. I had not been in contact with Tom for a long time. He was talking about a trip to Israel and said he had a few openings. I immediately got on the phone and called him. It was good to hear his voice once again. I first met Tom on the Tyler YWAM campus at a planning session for their annual Go Fest, a weekend festival designed to encourage people to go on a mission trip. They asked me to be one of the daytime speakers. Tom used his radio program to spread the news about the event.

As I listened to Tom talk about the trip that day, I felt the Holy Spirit nudge me to go with Tom. I asked him to reserve a spot for me on his trip. He sounded really excited to hear from me, since I had not talked to him in a long time. He immediately said, "I will give you a $200 discount for the trip." So I made a trip to the Holy Land. Two of the most exciting times on that trip were the boat ride across the Sea of Galilee, and when Tom asked me to assist him in baptizing folks in the Jordan River. Meanwhile, as we ministered at New Life Worship Center, we watched it grow from about 200 members to over 1,300 members. They built a new, beautiful, modern sanctuary outside the city of Tyler. After pastoring the senior adults for a while, my wife and I moved on to a different assignment. We took charge of intercessory prayer and pastoral care. I also taught a Bible class on Wednesday nights. God was good to us and allowed us to continue to minister in our old age. One of my favorite scriptures is found in Psalm 92, where it says, "The righteous… shall still bear fruit in old age; they shall be fresh and flourishing." Margy remarked one day that it was the "eatingness" church we had ever been in. It seemed like there was a dinner every time you turned around, and I quickly gained weight. Soon Pastor Bond hired a new senior pastor and executive to him. He had formerly worked with Larry Lee at the Rock Church in Rockwall, Texas. I had already started in a nursing home ministry, so I stayed with that. The executive pastor later decided to take another job at an oil company, so Pastor Bond hired another executive pastor who also had worked with Larry Lee in the Rock Church. He was there approximately a year and he, too, left for another job. I never knew the reason.

I rode the waves of change and stayed with the church. Pastor Bond and his wife, CJ, were good to me and I felt I was where God put me, so there was no need to change. Although my pay had been reduced to one half, I seemed to manage all right. Pastor Bond told me I only needed to come into the office one day a week, but my job as pastoral care usually brought me into town three times per week. I soon acquired a team to work in the nursing home with Margy and me. AJ and Margie Johnson, a therapist and his wife who worked in nursing homes, loved the ministry. They, along with Sister Ella Prince, became our faithful nursing-home team. I never had to worry about those three faithful servants. Actually, at that time, we were considered volunteer staff. On Sundays, we would hold a one-hour service from 3 p.m. to 4 p.m. We would sing, preach, and pray for all the participants. We quickly made friends at Claremont, Azalea Place, and the Hamptons nursing homes. We also worked at Reunion Plaza for a while. One of the ladies at the nursing home that we became friends with was Annie Smith. She was 100 years old when we met her, and she died at 102. She loved God and was well liked at their community church. They honored her at her funeral, which I attended.

Then there was Eunice, who was 99 years old. She was a special child of God, always smiling and thankful for any blessing. She died at 100 years old. I don't think either of these old saints had any relatives. They probably outlived them all.

Another special person that we met at Azalea Place was Marshall Bond. He had just recently had a leg amputated because of several infected spider bites. We were having a service and I noticed that he had tears in his eyes. Marshall was just in his late 50s. We prayed for him and later that week I kept thinking about him, so I went back to pay a personal visit. Marshall had a lot of physical struggles. He later had to have his other leg amputated. I visited him often in the nursing home and at the hospital. I continued to pray for him and encourage him, and at times he would do well. During the battle with his health, I met his daughter who had recently been released from prison. Marshall soon lost the battle for his life, but not before he was reunited with his Maker. The family asked me to officiate at his funeral. These are just a few of the people we met while ministering at the nursing home. I became well aware of death, but for all, we tried to bring hope of eternal life through Jesus Christ.

CHAPTER 15
My Life, My Wife

AS I CLOSE this story, I have two regrets in my life. Number one, I wish I had surrendered to God earlier in life. Number two, I wish I had prayed more with my children as they were growing up, and read the word more together as a family. I've never reached the top of the mountain, or what the world would call success. I have not experienced fame in any measure. But I've learned to be content in whatever state I find myself. I thank God for my simple life in the valley. I love the old hymn that says, "When you walk with the Lord in the light of His word, what a glory He sheds on our way. When we do His good will, He abides with us still, and with all who will trust and obey." That's the only way to be happy!

At the time of this writing, Margy and I have been married over 60 years. The old saying, "Time goes by fast when you're having fun," is certainly true. God has surely blessed me with a wonderful wife. She has been a wonderful example of a very caring wife and mother. She has displayed unconditional love for me and for our family. She has been very forgiving of all my shortcomings and insecurities and my love for her has grown deeper through the years. We have had our ups and downs, but the ups were more frequent than the downs. Without Jesus in our lives, it would never have lasted. We stand on the vows we made when we married. "Till death do us part." Amen.

The life of an ordinary man was not an easy life, but it was fruitful. There were many difficult times, but I learned, as Paul did, to be content in whatever state I was in. When I say learned, it doesn't mean I didn't struggle, but I believe the struggles we go through in life are what make us who we are. One of my favorite scriptures is Psalm 84:5-7:

> "Blessed is the man whose strength is in you, whose heart is set on pilgrimage, as they pass through the valley of Baca, they make it a spring; the rain covers it with pools. They go from strength to strength; each one appears before God in Zion (Psalm 84: 5-7)."

The Valley of Baca could be any difficulty that we go through in life. How we respond to these difficulties is what shapes our life.

Open Letters to My Children

AS I WAS bringing this portion of my life to an end, I felt I should write an open letter to my children and grandchildren.

Dear Mike,

You were the cutest baby on earth when you were born. It was a joy to watch you grow up. You always seemed to have a much-submitted spirit. I don't ever remember hearing you speak a rebellious word. I remember one occasion when you were asked over to a young girl's house for lunch. She was a girl that hung out at the swimming pool where you were a lifeguard. You came to me one day and asked me for permission to go to her house for lunch. I asked you if her parents were home and you said they weren't at home. I felt a check in my spirit and told you that the devil walks about like a roaring lion looking for someone to devour. I followed up with; I don't think that would be wise. You readily accepted my counsel and no more was said. Later in the year that girl turned up pregnant. I believe by your submission to me, your father, you avoided what could have been a serious problem.

I have always been proud of you and your talented accomplishments. When I saw you in Bye-bye Birdie, and Ginger Brook Fare, and Music Machine I could hardly believe the God- given talent you had. It made me very proud. Also, when you were successful as a car salesman in providing for your family, I was proud. Yes! There were times when I was disappointed and hurt over some of the directions you chose, but I never stopped loving you. Love, your Dad

Dear Cindy,

What a joy you were to watch growing up. I thought I had the cutest little girl in the whole world. I loved to watch you playing in the mud. I even loved you very much when you resisted very strongly any correction, like a spanking. As you were growing up, you seemed to have a wit about you that spoke of wisdom beyond your years. You never seemed to get goo-goo eyes for all of the boys that a lot of teenage girls did, but you always seemed to enjoy life. It was a pleasure to watch you playing sports such as basketball and volleyball; I don't think I missed a game. And later on, becoming a mother and raising such talented children—what a blessing that was. I know you managed well on a very limited income. I often wished our business could have afforded to pay you and Aaron more money. And now! A nurse and a grandmother; now enjoying some of the blessings that were limited on your meager income at Gateway Fence Company. I love you very much and always will. I am very proud to have you and Aaron living close to us. That is a blessing that I thank God for every day. Also, Aaron, I am very proud to have you as my son-in-law. Love always, Dad

Dear Brian,

My mind goes back to the day you were born. I remember praying daily for you to overcome the respiratory problem you were born with. I think you lived for five days in an incubator, while your mother and I prayed for you each day. Then, I watched you grow up, tall and strong and even bigger than Mike. I enjoyed our wrestling matches until you got too big for me to handle. Then came the football games and track meets that I thoroughly enjoyed watching. I sometimes had to make a four-hour trip from Houston to Lindale to see a game, but I never regretted it. Brian, I have always been proud of you no matter what you were doing to earn a living. There were times I was hurt and disappointed in some of your occupational decisions, but I never stopped loving you. Now, you and Jennifer have blessed us with the most adorable little grandsons one could ask for. Thank you both for allowing us to be such a close part of the family. I love you, Brian, I always have and I always will. Love, your Dad

To all my grandchildren,

I love you very much; you have brought much joy and happiness to me. I am so thankful to God that he has kept our family close together. I pray for you daily, that God would keep you healthy and strong. I pray that the devil does not have his way in your life and that you may find the joy in the Lord that your grandmother and I have found. Love always, Grandpa Sonny

My Core Beliefs

AFTER YEARS OF pursuing God and seeking His will for my life, I have come to what I call my core beliefs. These beliefs have come about through much study and prayer and seeking the will of God for my life. I pray that whoever reads these beliefs will do so prayerfully for revelation and not for debate. I definitely believe in deathbed repentance. The thief on the cross is one good example. Jesus said, "This day thou shalt be with me in paradise."

I believe God is a merciful God who is not willing that any should perish, but all should come to repentance. I believe that God will take a good look at the intentions of a person and weigh out his whole life. I do not believe that everything is predetermined as the Calvinist believes, but every man or woman is given many opportunities to come to Jesus. I do believe we are predestined to a purpose, and that purpose is to become like His Son. Romans 8:28-29 says, "And we know that all things work together for good to those who love God, to those who are called according to His purpose. For whom He foreknew, He also predestined to be conformed to the image of His Son, that he might be the firstborn among many brethren." When we receive Jesus as our Lord and Savior, He begins a work of changing us into His image, line upon line, precept upon precept. I believe that God knows all the possibilities because He has all the knowledge. I believe because of this knowledge, He can predict with accuracy what the future holds. But, it is not predetermined. If it were, then we would have no free will and love as a choice would not exist. I do not believe that once a man is saved he cannot lose his salvation, but I do not believe that it is as easy to lose, as some would believe. I believe that if a man refuses to repent, he becomes harder and harder in his heart. If the hardening of his heart continues without revival and he once again becomes a habitual sinner, then when he dies he faces eternal judgment. One thing I have noticed over the years of ministry I have been involved with is that if a person refuses to humble himself and repent, he may create a God that fits into whatever he wants to believe. I believe that every Christian should be committed to a local church for the fellowship and the covering it offers. You have never seen a finger walking around by itself (See 1 Corinthians 12:12-25). I believe that every Christian should be obedient with his finances and pay his tithes and offerings to the local church. I also believe the believer should be open to the leading of the Spirit to give to missions and other charitable organizations. "For I am the Lord, I do not change; therefore you are not consumed, O sons of Jacob. Yet from the days of your fathers you have gone away from My ordinances, and have not kept them. Return to Me, and I will return to you, says the Lord of hosts. But you said, 'In what way shall we return?' Will a man rob God? Yet you have robbed Me! But you say, 'In what have we robbed you?' In tithes and offerings. You are cursed with a curse, for you have robbed Me, even this whole nation. Bring all the tithes into the storehouse, that there may be food in My house, and try Me in this, says the Lord of hosts, if I will not open for you the windows of heaven and pour out for you such a blessing that there will not be room enough to receive it" (Malachi 3: 6-11). I believe that God is a prayer-answering God and that " …men always ought to pray and not lose heart" (Luke 18:1). I believe in divine healing of the body and soul. I believe that "… without faith, it is impossible to please Him" (Hebrews 11:6).

I believe that belief and obedience are synonymous in the Bible. To believe in God is not just giving mental assent to the fact that He exists, but one must have a heart to do what He says. "If you love Me, keep My commandments" (John 14:15). James 2:17 says, "Thus also faith by itself, if it does not have works, is dead. But someone will say, 'You have faith, and I have works.' Show me your faith without your works, and I will show you my faith by my works. You believe that there is one God. You do well. Even the demons believe—and tremble! But do you want to know, O foolish man, that faith without works is dead?" We don't work to obtain faith; we work because we have faith. That's quite a difference. The Bible also says in 1 Peter 1:15, "but as He who called you is holy, you also be holy in all your conduct, because it is written, 'Be holy, for I am holy.'" I believe that holiness is not necessarily the way you dress, but it is a reflection of walking in the light as He is in the light. Simply put, living up to the light you have.

I believe that the gifts of the Spirit are as relevant today as they were in the book of Acts. I do not believe that the gift is a sign of spiritual maturity though; love is the ultimate sign of maturity. Gifts are given to babies that they may become mature, not because they are mature.

In the early 70s, I was involved with the charismatic movement. I helped start a chapter of the Full Gospel Businessmen's organization. We quickly grew from 25 to over 200 men in our once-a-month services. We would have worship and testimonies, along with a main speaker. Many were touched by God and filled with the Holy Spirit. There were some troubling things in this movement that caused me to wonder about its legitimacy. God began to show me the error with the charismatic movement was that they tried to jump from grace to power without discipline and holiness. They assumed that a demonstration of gifts was a sign of maturity, when in reality they were just babes. It is no accident that the love chapter is sandwiched between gifts and the law governing the gifts. Paul said, "… earnestly desire the best gifts. And yet I show you a more excellent way. Though I speak with the tongues of men and angels, but have not love, I have become sounding brass or a clanging cymbal" (1 Corinthians 12:31-13:1).

Love is the evidence that one is mature.

Another thing that troubled me for years is the doctrine that says the evidence of being filled with the Holy Spirit is speaking in tongues. I believe the true evidence is the fruit of the Spirit. "… love, joy, peace, longsuffering, kindness, goodness, faithfulness, gentleness, self- control" (Galatians 5:22). In 1 Corinthians 14:18-19, Paul said, "I thank my God that I speak with tongues more than you all; yet in church I would rather speak five words with my understanding, that I may teach others also, than 10,000 words in a tongue." I believe in the gift of tongues, but I do not believe that it is the initial evidence of being filled with the Holy Spirit. I've seen too many tongue-talking people that have no love. The Bible says you shall know them by their fruits. We have put people in places of maturity and given them authority when they are not ready, just because they operate in some gift. It has caused much confusion in the body of Christ.

One of the things that I find lacking in the body of Christ is the fear of the Lord. In a lot of churches, there is a doctrine going around that says you don't have to fear the Lord, because the Bible says perfect love casts out all fear (See 1 John 4:18). I believe that this Scripture is taken out of context to prove a doctrine that is not true. If we examine the whole of the Old Testament and the New Testament, we can find sufficient Scripture to prove that the fear of the Lord is the beginning of wisdom. Wisdom is seeing things from God's point of view, not from man's point of view.

So let's take a journey through some of the Old Testament Scripture along with the New Testament Scripture that backs up the fact that we should fear the Lord.

"The Lord is exalted, for He dwells on high; He has filled Zion with justice and righteousness. Wisdom and knowledge will be the stability of your times. And the strength of salvation; the fear of the Lord is His treasure" (Isaiah 33:5-6).

"Then Peter opened his mouth and said: 'In truth I perceive that God shows no partiality, but in every nation whoever fears Him and works righteousness is accepted by Him" (Acts 10:34-35).

"Men and brethren, sons of the family of Abraham, and those among you who fear God, to you the word of this salvation has been sent" (Acts 13:26).

"For as the heavens are high above the earth, so great is his mercy toward those who fear Him" (Psalm 103:11).

"Skilled living gets its start in the Fear-of-God insight into life from a knowing and all Holy God. It's through me, Lady Wisdom, that your life deepens, and the years of your life ripen" (Proverbs 9:10-11 from The Message Bible).

Let's look at some New Testament Scriptures that speak of the fear of the Lord.

"Therefore, having these promises, beloved, let us cleanse ourselves from all filthiness of the flesh and spirit, perfecting holiness in the fear of God" (2 Corinthians 7:1).

"And I say to you, my friends, do not be afraid of those who kill the body, and after that have no more that they can do. But I will show you whom you should fear: Fear Him who, after He has killed, has power to cast into hell; yes, I say to you, fear Him!" (Luke 12:4-5). This Scripture is printed in red letters, which means Jesus was speaking.

"Honor all people. Love the brotherhood. Fear God. Honor the king" (1 Peter 2:17). To honor someone means to esteem that person according to his or her true value. That value lies in the fact that we are created in the image of God. "Then God said, let us make man in Our image, according to Our likeness; and let them have dominion over the fish of the sea, and over the birds of the air, and over the cattle, and over all the earth and over every creeping thing that creeps on the earth" (Genesis 1:26).

I have shared some major scriptures that show we are to fear God. Now let us define the fear of the Lord. The original Greek words used for fear, in connection with the fear of the Lord, throughout most of the New Testament are phobos and phobeo. They generally mean "alarm, fright, or terror" and carry the idea of "being in awe of or having reverence." The fear of the Lord is produced in the soul by the Holy Spirit. Godly fear means we dread displeasing Him, desire his favor, revere His Holiness, submit to His will, are grateful for His benefits, sincerely worship Him, and conscientiously obey His Commandments. Great blessings are promised upon those who have it. Note: fear and love must coexist in us in order that both passions may be healthy and that we may please and rightly serve God.

The fear of the Lord includes:

- A profound and abiding respect and reverence of God and all things He declares holy
- Assigning God Most High the infinite and highest place of honor in your life
- Deeply appreciating the privilege of His presence and the wonder of His word
- Worshiping God alone with passionate praise and continual thanksgiving
- Honoring what He honors, loving what He loves, and hating what He hates
- Making His main thing our main thing
- Having an eternal yearning to please God and not offend Him
- Submitting your will to fully embrace His will

This tempering makes it impossible for the individual to sin casually or persistently.

The fear of the Lord is a cleansing or purifying agent that endures forever. It is a manifestation of the Holy Spirit and Jesus the Light. There is absolutely nothing corrupt or deceitful about it.

Now I will share some of the blessings of fearing God.

"How joyful are those who fear the Lord—all who follow his ways! You will enjoy the fruit of your labor. How joyful and prosperous you will be! Your wife will be like a fruitful grapevine, flourishing within your home. Your children will be like vigorous young olive trees as they sit around your table. That is the Lord's blessing for those who fear Him" (Psalm 128:1-4 NLT).

"Blessed (happy, fortunate, and to be envied) is the man who reverently and worshipfully fears (the Lord) at all times (regardless of the circumstances)…" (Proverbs 28:14 Amplified Bible).

"Oh, how great is Your goodness, which You have laid up for those who fear you, which You have prepared for those who trust in You in the presence of the sons of men!" (Psalm 31:19).

This study on the fear of the Lord is not an exhaustive study, but I hope that it creates an interest in someone to completely study this subject.

I love the fact that all men are created in the image of God, but I hate the fact that we can destroy that image by our lifestyle. I believe plainly that God gives favor to those who put their trust in Him. "But let all those rejoice who put their trust in You; let them ever shout for joy, because You defend them; let those who love Your name be joyful in You. For You, O Lord, will bless the righteous; with favor you will surround him as with a shield" (Psalm 5:11-12). I believe when we trust God, He puts a godly wall around us.

There's a lot said today about tolerance versus intolerance. The Liberals think the Republicans are intolerable. The Republicans think the Liberals are intolerable. The sinner thinks the Christian is intolerable, because they are against homosexuality or same-sex marriage. The Christian thinks the sinner is intolerable, because they want to take the subject of God from everything. It's hard to know which one is the most tolerable or intolerable. All I know is that God does not tolerate sin. He may forgive sin, but he always says, go and sin no more lest a greater thing come upon you. (John 5:14) So just what is sin? Let me define sin as I have learned in the 54 years that I have served God. Sin is the voluntary state in which emotional gratification is made the supreme concern. We can simplify that definition with one word: selfishness. Another definition that needs to be clarified is our definition for the word love. In our English language, we use only one word for love. I love my dog, I love pizza, I love watermelon, and I love my wife. We use the same word for all these things. The Greeks have several words for love, and all with different meanings. So let's start with the Greek word, ***phileo***, a warm affectionate love. It resides primarily in the feeling. This is where we get the word Philadelphia, the city of brotherly love. Another great word for love is ***estorge***; this too is a warm affectionate feeling. Then we have the Greek word ***eros***, a word that has to do with sexual love. It too resides primarily in the feeling. Lastly, we have the Greek word ***agape***. This is a spiritual love, which comes from God to us. This is a love of the will; it gives without expecting anything in return. It is an unselfish choice for the highest good of the one you are willing to love.

"For God so loved the world that He gave His only begotten Son, that whoever believes in Him should not perish but have everlasting life" (John 3:16).

One of my favorite scriptures is Psalm 147:10-11: "He does not delight in the strength of the horse; He takes no pleasure in the legs of a man. The Lord takes pleasure in those who fear Him, in those who hope in His mercy." I always say, "I am stuck like a dope with a thing called hope."

Another one of my favorite scriptures is found in Psalm 145:17-19: "The Lord is righteous in all His ways, gracious in all His works. The Lord is near to all who call upon Him, to all who call upon Him in truth. He will fulfill the desire of those who fear Him; He also will hear their cry and save them."

One thing that has concerned me over the years is the current trend in our world to legitimize the sin of homosexuality. Since the Bible is very explicit concerning this unnatural practice, I have made it a point to study the lives of prominent people in society and those I have come in contact with in my own ministry. It seems they all have similar patterns in their background. While at Brownsville school of Ministry, I wrote an article concerning this subject and it was published in a book written by a friend on staff. The book is titled So Free by Bill Suddeth, and the following is that article:

Pattern for Homosexual Behavior
by Sonny Jaynes

The doorway into that lifestyle usually begins in the early years before young adulthood or adolescence. Some factors are a father's rejection either by divorce, or just plain neglect, and usually an overprotective mother that is very controlling. Since there is no intimacy with the child by the father, the child begins to be confused about his true identity. Before the Industrial Revolution, this was rarely a problem since young boys spent most of their daylight hours working on the farm with their fathers. Perhaps there might have been a sexual encounter during the early steps of puberty. This could happen in an innocent exploratory way, since a lot of children have had no instruction by the parents to prepare them for the changes they are to encounter. It could also be something forced on them by someone older, perhaps even a close relative. Since there is no open communication with the parents, it is kept secret; this then leads to further confusion. This encounter could be easily mistaken for the love they are missing, since it gives them some form of gratification. Then possibly, a sexual encounter in high school or college with the same sex could have occurred. This is easier to fall into since there has already been a previous experience. This leaves an open door for more confusion and allows the devil access into the life of the persons involved, planting seeds of doubt as to their own sexual identity. If repented at this stage, there can be total freedom. There must be a Spirit-led witness in love and understanding in order for the seed to grow. Since the heart is very hard at this point, only love and understanding can break the hard ground. Any attempt to blast or harshly rebuke will just result in further hardening the person. As sexual contact is continued, the person becomes more and more obsessed with sexual gratification. This leads to deeper and deeper bondage. The longer a person is involved with this lifestyle, the less chance of change.

In Matthew 6:33, God says, "But seek first the kingdom of God and His righteousness, and all these things shall be added to you."

The kingdom of God is where the King has authority. If He reigns in your heart, then you are His kingdom. If He is your King, then you must obey Him. So, you must seek to let His righteousness rule your life. Not what you think is righteousness, but what He thinks is righteousness.

When that is the priority in your life, then He will give you what you need—not what you want or what the world thinks you need to be happy. The person who seeks his own happiness in life will never find it. When you seek God and the blessings of others first, then happiness is yours as a byproduct. In Job 42:10 God says, "And the Lord restored Job's losses when he prayed for his friends."

There is a lot said these days about success. I believe Jesus gives us the keys to real success in Matthew 5:

- "Blessed are the poor in spirit," those who know their need for God.
- "Blessed are those who mourn," because they know their selfish choices have broken God's heart.
- "Blessed are the meek," those who have yielded their will to meet His will.

- "Blessed are those who hunger and thirst for righteousness." Do you hunger to fit His criteria? Then you will be filled.

- "Blessed are the merciful, for they shall receive mercy." These are the people who have such compassion that they can sow Spiritual seeds in their enemy's field.

- "Blessed are the peacemakers," those who are willing to work hard to bring peace. There is a difference between a peacekeeper and a peacemaker. The peacemaker will not sacrifice God's standards to keep peace; one is a pacifist, the other a warrior.

- "Blessed are those who are willing to lay down their life for the kingdom of God. For theirs is the kingdom of heaven." I believe we must be witnesses wherever we go and whatever we do. As one great man of God said, "And sometimes use words."

The Bible says, "Therefore if the Son makes you free, you shall be free indeed" (John 8:36). But freedom and blessing come with responsibility.

Let me quote the late, great orator from Britain, Edmund Burke: "Men are qualified for civil liberty in exact proportion to their disposition to put moral chains upon their own appetites; in proportion as their love of justice is above their rapacity; in proportion as their soundness and sobriety of understanding is above their vanity and presumption; in proportion as they are more disposed to listen to the counsel of the wise and good, in preference to the flattery of the knaves. Society cannot exist, unless a controlling power upon will and appetite be placed somewhere; and the less of it there is within, the more there must be without. It is ordained in the eternal Constitution of things, that men of intemperate minds cannot be free. Their passions forge their fetters."

In his book, America Is Too Young to Die, Leonard Ravenhill said, "America can die, but it would have to be by suicide. It would be because she thinks God is dead, and because she believes that His laws, which when broken have felled every nation that ever lived, do not, in her hour of freedom and influence, include her." He also said, "America fights a battle that cannot be won at the ballot box. Her need is not the 'new morality' of the hour, but new morals based on the old laws of God."

We must stop playing church; we must be salt and light. Our programs will not touch the people's heart; only our lives dedicated to God will influence man. We must stay on our knees before God for direction and not be looking to what works in other churches. It is better to have 200 dedicated people who are willing to take up their cross and follow Jesus, than 2,000 attendees who are not sincere followers.

There Is No Gain But By a Loss, a hymn written by Arthur S. Booth-Clibborn, had a personal impact on my life.

> *There is no gain but by a loss;*
> *We cannot save but by the cross,*
> *The corn of wheat, to multiply*
> *Must fall into the ground and die;*
> *O should a soul alone remain*
> *When it a hundredfold can gain?*
> *Wherever you ripe fields behold,*
> *Waving to God their sheaves of gold,*
> *Be sure some corn of wheat has died,*
> *Some saintly soul been crucified;*
> *Someone has suffered, wept and prayed,*
> *And fought hell's legions undismayed (Booth-Clibborn, 1918).*

Although I have not excelled as a pulpit minister, there have been times when God has given me a special message. I would like to include a few of those special messages that I believe came from God.

After careful study of the moral government of God, I believe the true paradigm shift that Jesus wishes is to turn from religion to love, and from judgment to love. But true love has government and government has laws. Before man can receive mercy that leads to pardon, he must first be guilty. Only the guilty can receive mercy. "And Jesus said, 'For judgment I have come into this world, that those who do not see may see, and that those who see may be made blind'" (John 9:39).

"For unto us a child is born, unto us a Son is given; and the government will be upon His shoulder. And His name will be called Wonderful, Counselor, Mighty God, Everlasting Father, Prince of Peace. Of the increase of His government and peace there will be no end, upon the throne of David and over His kingdom, to order it and establish it with judgment and justice from that time forward, even forever. The zeal of the Lord of hosts will perform this" (Isaiah 9:6-7 KJV).

We are living in a time of easy believe-ism and cheap grace. There needs to be a serious reassessment of a modern theology, which preaches a salvation without submission, a discipleship without discipline, reconciliation without repentance, and a love without a conscience or fear of the consequences of sin. What would happen if all our cities had no red lights and no speed signs and no stripes dividing our lanes or directing our traffic? If there is to be order and a just way of life for a world full of people, there must be a uniform moral code for all to abide by. Biblical Christianity presents such a system, and the moral laws of God are given us in Exodus 20. However, with any law, there must be a sanction or a consequence. Without consequences, law would be mere advice.

Let me quote from the National Commission on the Causes and Prevention of Violence in 1969: "...order is indispensable to society, law is indispensable to order, and enforcement is indispensable to law" (To Establish Justice, To Insure Domestic Tranquility, Final report of the National Commission on the Causes and Prevention of Violence, 1969, p.142).

The atoning death of Jesus can only make our forgiveness possible if we repent of our sin and make Him our Savior and Lord through a commitment of faith.

What is moral government? It is the benevolent effort of a loving Creator to regulate the conduct of moral creatures so they can fulfill their planned purpose.

What is the moral law? In its most general sense, it is a rule of action. Moral government must function under the principle of moral law. Moral law does not determine action but describes what action ought to be chosen for the happiness of all.

How does moral law differ from physical law? Moral law is a law for action, while physical law is a rule of action. One operates by free will; the other operates by cause and effect.

Free choice is the distinctive characteristic of moral government. While God exerts every influence upon man's personality, consistent with man's moral freedom, to get him to make the right choices, in no sense is God the cause of man's moral choices for which he is held accountable.

It is God's obligation to govern; it is our obligation to be governed. God fulfilled his obligation in love or disinterested benevolence. To be governed is all He asked us to do. The moral law itemizes in a ten-fold way our moral obligation: the first four commandments show our obligation toward God and the last six our obligation toward our fellow man. The Lord Jesus summarizes our moral obligation in a twofold way. "'Teacher, which is the great commandment in the law?' Jesus said to him, 'You shall love the Lord your God with all your heart, and with all your soul, and with all your mind. This is the first and great commandment. And the second is like it. You shall love your neighbor as yourself. On these two commandments hang all the Law and the Prophets" (Matthew22:36-40).

The apostle Paul, by inspiration, summarized this moral obligation to both God and man by one word, 'love,' which is a voluntary state of impartial goodwill toward all moral beings. "Owe no one anything except to love one another, for he who loves another has fulfilled the law. For the Commandments, 'You shall not commit adultery,' 'You shall not murder,' 'You shall not steal,' 'You shall not bear false witness,' 'You shall not covet,' and if there is any other commandment, are all summed up in this saying, namely, 'You shall love your neighbor as yourself'" (Romans13:8-10).

"For you, brethren, have been called to liberty; only do not use liberty as an opportunity for the flesh, but through love serve one another. For all the law is fulfilled in one word, even in this: 'You shall love your neighbor as yourself.' But if you bite and devour one another, beware lest you be consumed by one another!" (Galatians5:13-15).

"Now the purpose of the commandment is love from a pure heart, from a good conscience, and from sincere faith" (1 Timothy1:5).

One Sunday morning at Community Christian Fellowship, while listening to the speaker, the question arose in my mind concerning bringing glory to God and I began to ponder that question. Once again the Holy Spirit spoke to me. I wrote down exactly what I felt the Holy Spirit was telling me.

"God's glory is manifested through a display of His character and reputation as represented in the life of those who are born again through the resurrection power and grace from the Holy Spirit. The power of God fell in the upper room on the day of Pentecost and those that received became witnesses, or martyrs, to display the same strength of character that was demonstrated by Jesus Christ.

"This simply means that men would display the character and power of Christ as they went about doing the ordinary things of life. There would be a sense of fulfillment knowing that they were displaying the reputation and character of the Lord in their everyday duties. This would be a powerful witness, since the world could not know the joy of Jesus in the mundane.

"Women would display the same zeal and strength of character in their womanly duties, finding it a great joy to make their families happy and taken care of. They would display high levels of energy in order to fulfill the Proverbs 31 example of a godly mother and wife.

"When our lives are truly examples to the world of what God intended them to be, then He is glorified." Verification of this word is found in 2 Thessalonians 1:1-12.

Oswald Chambers says, "True earnestness is founded in obeying God, not in the inclination to serve him that is born of undisciplined human nature. It is inconceivable, but true nevertheless, that Saints are not bringing every project into captivity, but are doing work for God at the instigation of their own human nature, which has not been spiritualized by determined discipline" (Excerpt from My Utmost for His Highest, September 9th).

I've not been one to receive many prophetic dreams or prophetic words, but I would like to share this particular word that came to me strongly. I was at a special meeting with Brother

Leonard Ravenhill, and about 20 other ministers from the Lindale and Dallas area. Besides Brother Ravenhill, there were Rick Joyner, Paul Cain, and Mike Bickel. These leaders were sitting at a table in front of us. There was no music, and no special sermon. These four men simply shared their vision of what was coming in the future. The meeting lasted over four hours. I was receiving so much in my spirit that the tears were flowing down my cheeks. God was speaking to me through these men. When I left that meeting I did not have words to describe what God was speaking to me, so I went home and went to my study and began to pray. I said, "God, please help me put into words what I felt the Spirit speaking to me during that meeting. The following is what I wrote down.

January 26, 1989

God is going to raise up a new breed of not only ministers, but leaders. They will be unified by selflessness, not by ideals but by The Ideal (Jesus). It will not have the mark of human effort. It will not spring forth out of the tree of knowledge of good and evil, but out of the Tree of Life, Jesus. Too many have been converted out of the tree of knowledge, and not from the Tree of Life. Too many are converted by man. There is a fundamental deception in the body of Christ. We are emphasizing who we are in Christ. That has been over emphasized; it is man centered. We cannot get to Jesus any other way but by the cross. The emphasis should be who He is in us. When the fire of judgment comes it will weld believers together. No longer will there be a halting between two opinions as the Israelites in the presence of Elijah and the prophets of Baal, when they answered not a word. Baal represents worldliness. There is an unholy mixture in the church. In the fiery judgment everything false will be consumed. It takes extreme heat to weld, but when the weld is completed it is stronger than the thing that is being welded. These new relationships between men and women of God will be bonded as that kind of weld. No longer will Christianity be a system to line up our doctrines properly; it will be an encounter with Christ, Himself. The Son of Man is still looking for a place to lay His head.

Now the Scripture I referenced in the beginning, Isaiah 4:3-4 says, "And it shall come to pass that he who is left in Zion and remains in Jerusalem will be called holy—everyone who is recorded among the living in Jerusalem. When the Lord has washed away the filth of the daughters of Zion, and purged the blood of Jerusalem from her midst, by the spirit of judgment and by the spirit of burning...."

Also, Isaiah 26:9-10 says, "With my soul I have desired You in the night, yes, by my spirit within me I will seek You early; for when Your judgments are in the earth, the inhabitants of the world will learn righteousness. Let grace be shown to the wicked, yet he will not learn righteousness; in the land of uprightness he will deal unjustly, and will not behold the majesty of the Lord."

On September 11, 2001, I was watching the news on TV when the twin towers of the World Trade Center were destroyed by terrorists. Our country had not witnessed such an invasion since Pearl Harbor was attacked by the Japanese. That morning, I had a chapel service with the students and B.R.S.M. I told them this was a wake-up call to America. I am now reading the book called The Harbinger by Jonathan Cahn, a Messianic Jew. Cahn reveals the secrets of America's future as reflected in the prophecies in Chapter 9 of Isaiah. The prophecy that God gave me in 1989 became more realistic in the near future. When

I gave my life to Jesus, I was radically changed. That rebirth started me on my journey to the Promised Land. I left youthful lust and started a life of service for the King and His kingdom. While I know not everyone who claims to be a Christian really is one, I do believe that as a Christian, I am obligated to stand up for Christian values and to vote in free elections based on my Christian worldview. I do believe that if a person claims to be a Christian, he or she should automatically reject homosexuality as a lifestyle. They should stand up for traditional marriage as being between a man and a woman. I believe we should read the Bible for revelation by the Holy Spirit, and not for debate.

How do you debate Jesus' own words in John 14:6, "I am the way, the truth, and the life. No one comes to the Father except through Me," or in verse 21, "He who has My commandments and keeps them, it is he who loves Me. And he who loves Me will be loved by My Father, and I will love him and manifest myself to him."

I believe we should only trust God to reveal the word to us, and He will. I believe, "…if we walk in the light as He is in the light, we have fellowship one with another and the blood of Jesus His Son will cleanse us from all sin. If we say we have no sin, we deceive ourselves, and the truth is not in us" (1 John 1:7-8). John is talking about momentary acts of selfishness, not a lifestyle. He also says in verse 9, "If we confess our sins, He is faithful and just to forgive us our sins and to cleanse us from all unrighteousness."

To walk in the light means to obey God as he reveals His word to us. I find that many so- called Christians study the word to find excuses for their sin. As the Bible says in Matthew 23:12, we must humble ourselves under the mighty hand of God that He may exalt us. "Casting all our care upon Him for He cares for us" (1 Peter 5: 7).

How do we get that light? "But as it is written: Eye has not seen, nor ear heard, nor have entered into the heart of man the things which God has prepared for those who love Him. But God has revealed them to us through His Spirit. For the Spirit searches all things, yes, the deep things of God. For what man knows the things of man except the spirit of man which is in him?" (1 Corinthians 2:9-11).

I believe that God wants to have an intimate relationship with us. Church on Sundays is not enough for us to enter into that kind of relationship. We need daily prayer and devotion. I believe our prayers should be more of penetrating the heart of God, rather than trying to persuade Him. We must touch Him by being totally honest with Him. We don't need to persuade God how spiritual we are, because He already knows. As we approach God in humility and brokenness, He will listen. I believe our prayer life should be more listening than talking! Sometimes we spend so much time trying to convince God of our wants and needs, that He can't get a word in. Intimacy with God is like intimacy with our spouse. We need to listen with all our hearts and not just our ears. Prayer and worship go hand in hand. We enter His gates with thanksgiving. Praise gets us through the gates and past the outer courts, but worship gets us into the Holiest of Holies. When we get there, we are by ourselves with God. There's no one in there but you and God. That's where there is rest. One minute in His presence is worth any effort we put forth to get there. Let me share with you briefly what it's taken me a lifetime to find out. This was revealed to me while reading one of A. W. Tozer's books. This is how to develop spiritual aloneness:

1. Find a private spot to be alone with God.
2. Stay in that spot until all the surrounding noises begin to fade out of your heart and a sense of God's presence envelops you.

3. Listen to the inward voice until you learn to recognize it.
4. Stop trying to compete with others.
5. Give yourself to God and then be what and who you are without regard to what others think. Stop pretending.
6. Reduce your interests to what benefits you spiritually. Don't try to know what will be of no service to you. (See Ecclesiastes12:12-14.)
7. Learn to pray inwardly every moment. After a while, you can do this even while you work.
8. Practice candor, childlike honesty, and humility.

I believe if you put this into practice with an honest and sincere heart, you will hear from God.

As I close this book and this chapter of my life, there are many things on my mind I would like to express to those who would listen. Our country is in serious trouble; our nation is divided as I have never seen it before. At the time of this writing, our two political parties are in a serious debate over what is best for the country. The so-called Progressive Liberals are interested in a country that is led primarily by government. They seem to want to lead us into a socialistic form of government, where government is in control of almost everything. If you know anything about the Constitution, you will see this is totally contrary to the Founding Fathers' intentions for our nation. In just a little over 200 years, we grew to be a superpower for good in the world. America has contributed more money to missionaries that spread the gospel throughout the world than any other country. But this liberty is being threatened by the dominating power of the Liberal party. Not only is our monetary system being threatened, but also our freedom of religion is being challenged. The Muslims are gaining strength in our nation. Recently, our president acknowledged how the Muslims have contributed so much to our nation's greatness, while at the same time ignoring our National Day of Prayer.

Books That Have Helped Define Me

I HAVE ENJOYED READING many spiritually inspiring books in my life, and I have tried not to read a lot of books that had no spiritual impact on me. Most of the time, I was too busy to read just for entertainment. I have compiled a list of the books that have impacted my life. Of course, the main book is the Holy Bible, especially the New King James Version. Here are a few of those books:

Systematic Theology by Charles Finney

It all adds up to love by J.W. Jepson

The Cost of Discipleship by Dietrich Bonheoffer

Sharing your faith: The 3 M's of witnessing by Gordon Olson

Why Pray: Lessons Learned in the School of Prayer by B. J. Willhite

Unto Full Stature by DeVern Fromke

The Integrity Crisis by Warren Wiersbe

My Utmost for His Highest by Oswald Chambers

Why Revival Tarries by Leonard Ravenhill

Sit, Walk, Stand by Watchmen Nee

God at War: The Bible & Spiritual Conflict by Gregory Boyd

The Clash of the Kingdoms by Steve Harrison

The Pursuit of God by A. W. Tozer

Revival: Principles to Change the World by Winkie Pratney

America Is Too Young to Die by Leonard Ravenhill

The Complete Collection of E. M. Bounds on Prayer

Book one: The Necessity of prayer

Book Two: The Essentials of Prayer

Book three: The Possibilities of Prayer

Book four: The Reality of Prayer

Man: The Dwelling Place of God by A. W. Tozer

In His Steps by Charles Sheldon

Deeper Experiences of Famous Christians by James Gilchrist Lawson

Youth Aflame: Manual for Discipleship by Winkie Pratney

Revival by Martin Lloyd-Jones

These are some of the books that have impacted my life. I could probably list many more, but if you read these you will have a storehouse of spiritual treasures.

In Closing

TO GOD BE the glory, my prayer is that I might share something that will inspire you to dedicate your life to the Lord Jesus Christ. He has made my life worth living and I owe it all to Him.

One of my favorite passages of Scripture is found in Matthew 25:14-30, "For the kingdom of heaven is like a man traveling to a far country, who called his own servants and delivered his goods to them. And to one he gave five talents, to another two, and to another one, to every man according to his own ability; and immediately he went on a journey. Then he who had received the five talents went and traded with them, and made another five talents. And likewise he who had received two gained two more also. But he who had received one went and dug in the ground, and hid his lord's money."

I'm sure that most of you have read this parable. I feel like I am the man with the one talent, while using a good work ethic and a strong desire to do whatever God asked. I believe that whether we have one talent or many, when we use them for God, He will bless us. I know people with multiple talents who don't use them for God, and they produce no fruit for His kingdom. I know that my children and grandchildren have been given many talents. My prayers are that they use them for the glory of God.

"…be steadfast, immovable, always abounding in the work of the Lord, knowing that your labor is not in vain" (1 Corinthians15:58). Amen

Thank you, Jesus, for you have surely given me abundant life.

Lord, Light The Fire Again

LORD, WE ARE crying out, light the fire again. Lead us away from the clutches of materialism. Let Your holy truth ring from our hearts and not from our heads. Oh Lord, send the fire of passion for the lost. We need the fire of intent to live for You and not for our selfish pursuits.

Send the fire of holy desire and passionate love for You. Let the flames of holy love burn once again in our hearts.

Give us eyes to see the hypocrisy of our nation and its leaders. Give us the fire of holy boldness to stand up for what is good and righteous, no matter what the cost. Lord, we need the fires of revival. Send the fire of desire for holiness to our churches that will put out the flames of complacency. Lord, send the fire that will cause seeing eyes to be blind and blind eyes to see.

Lord, open the eyes of the leaders of our country to the truth of God's word. Raise up holy prophets that will speak the truth and not be concerned with how much the offering is.

Lord, forgive us for our laziness. Lord, forgive us for our godless pursuits and our prayer- less life. Forgive us for a lack of concern for the poor and lost souls. Lord, we need a fresh baptism of love for one another. We need a fresh baptism of commitment to our church and its ministries. Lord, we need you—not more programs. Please come and visit us with love and power. We are your weak and unmotivated church.

Lord, come quickly. Amen

Made in the USA
Columbia, SC
06 March 2019